ALL OVER THE MAP

An Extraordinary Atlas of the United States

featuring towns that actually exist!

by

David Jouris

1⊖

Ten Speed Press

Grate-acknowledgement for permission to reprint a portion of the lyrics from the following songs: • "My Little Town" Copyright © 1975 Paul Simon. Used by Permission of the Publisher. • "Blue Motel Room" (Joni Mitchell) © 1976 Crazy Crow Music. All Rights Reserved. Used by Permission. • "Political Science" (Randy Newman) © 1969 Six Continents Music Publishing, Inc. All Rights Reserved. Used by Permission. • "I've Got You Under My Skin" (Cole Porter) © 1936 Chappell & Co. (Renewed). All Rights Reserved. Used by Permission. • "Everyday I Write the Book" (Elvis Costello) © 1983 Plangent Vision Music Inc. (ASCAP). All Rights Reserved. Used by Permission. • Thank you. •

• This book was produced by Mandarin Offset in Hong Kong. Printed in Hong Kong. •

A number of the maps in this atlas originally appeared, in a somewhat similar form, although not with all of the same towns listed, in a recent series of black-and-white postcards produced by Hold the Mustard Productions at
P.O. Box 822   Berkeley
CA 94701   U.S.A.
Catalog $1.

1   2   3   4   5   6   7   —   00   99   98   97   96   95   94

AN ACKNOWLEDGED MAP

Gratitude

N

After the verb "To Love," "To Help" is
the most beautiful verb in the world!
—BARONESS BERTHA VON SUTTNER

ACKNOWLEDGMENTS

For their Assistance, Enthusiasm, Inspiration, and Kindness: thanks to Sally Aberg, Linda Allison, Andrea, James Barnes, Denise Bartout, Mariah Bear, Jeff Becom, Lilo Bloch, Liz Bordow, Linda Chester, Robin Chin, Judy, Tom, & Jennifer Connell, Fotofolio, Laurie Fox, Max Greenstreet, John Grimes, Thierry & Marie Hassoun, Chuck & Karla Herndon, Kristen Hoehler, David Holstrom, Fred Hyslop, Bill & Joanne Jouris, Don & Virginia Jouris, Maira Kalman, Virginia Kearns, Lazaris, David Loveall, Jackie Leventhal, Gunnar & Marcella Madsen, Lewis McArthur, Allen McKinney, Kirsty Melville, D. Patrick Miller, Tim Miller, Lisa Martine Pliscou, Patrick Ritter, Betsy & Ken Rock, Hebe Schafer, Gillian Silverman, Dan X. Solo, George Stewart, Iaen Sullivan, Donna Tiffany, Todd Walton, Bill Wells, Caroline White, George Young, plus some wonderfully helpful private citizens, archivists, historical societies, post offices, town halls, and a trove of libraries and librarians—including the Berkeley Public Library (especially Diane Davenport), the Library of Congress (especially Tanya Allison, Kathryn Engstrom, James Flatness, & Ronald Grim), & the Libraries of the University of California at Berkeley (especially the Map Room & Pacific Film Archive).

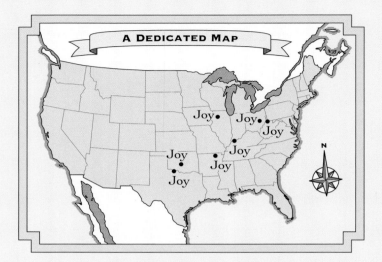

A DEDICATED MAP

Everyone in the world is looking for something and by means of maps each thing that is found is never lost again.
—RUSSELL HOBAN

For Joy

CONTENTS

N

I am still not convinced that I didn't
penetrate beyond geography.
—SAUL BELLOW

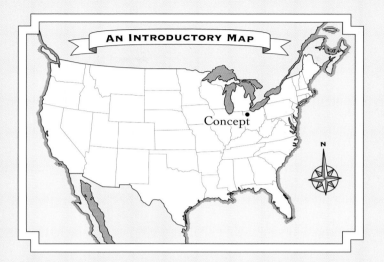

Maps are a way of organizing wonder.
—PETER STEINHART

INTRODUCTION

My Country 'Tis of Theme

It's not uncommon to hear people exclaim, "It's a small world!" To learn just how true this really is, take a look at "An Exotic Map." It reveals, for example, how one could start the day in Peru, be in Mexico for lunch, and drive leisurely across the border into Canada before nightfall. "An Exotic Map" is one of over thirty thematic maps in this atlas, which covers subjects ranging from sports to optimism to anatomy. The themes provide an inspired and sometimes zany perspective on the United States, uncovering some wonderful hidden treasures along the way.

The idea for these thematic maps began about seven years ago. I was thinking about how people get to the places they go in their lives—places like happiness or failure or contentment. I had an idea that it might be fun to illustrate the possibilities that a lifetime could hold by designing a map of sorts. The map would show the states of being that one might go through, presenting a variety of choices, en route to whatever destination one hoped for. At the time, I planned simply to make up the map, inventing names of places and putting them in some sort of seemingly random order. But when I looked at a real atlas, I found, to my surprise, there were a number of interestingly named towns that, while not fitting exactly to my original idea, held certain possibilities. Struck by the positive image created by towns like Confidence, CA; Delight, AR; and Prosperity, SC, I put together "An Optimistic Map."

Right from the beginning of my map work, a pattern emerged: every time I created a map, several new thematic possibilities introduced themselves. The makings for "A Pessimistic Map"—including Boring, OR; Dismal, TN; and Poverty, KY—appeared before "An Optimistic Map" was completed. Before all the "pessimistic" towns were assembled, names of animals and foreign cities caught my attention. And so it went, until I had more than 100 thematic map ideas in progress. One of my favorites is "A Curiously Juxtaposed Map." I enjoyed making connections between towns where, by and large, they were not originally foreseen. Sisters is located near Brothers in Oregon, Laurel near Hardy in Iowa, and Joy near Mudville (Casey isn't far away, either) in Texas.

Town names in the United States derive from a number of linguistic sources—mainly Native American languages, English, Spanish, and French. As evidenced by "A Latin Map," other languages have staked their claim too.

Some place-names came about as the result of misunderstanding, as is often the case with towns on "An Eccentric Map." Cheesequake, NJ, for example, was not named after an unsteady dessert, as some have suggested, but results from the attempt by non–Native Americans to say the word *chauquisitt* ("upland"). Similarly, Low Freight, AR, comes from the French *l'eau froide* ("cold water"). Names may also be altered by people who *do* know the original language. Trickem, AL, has nothing to do with deviousness; it derives from the fact that it is the site where three communities got together to build the Mt. Giliard Church, referred to as the "Three Communities' Church," or "Tri-Com," for short. From this, it was only a small step to Trickem.

Some communities are named after their founders, like Joes, CO, featured on "A Men's Map." Some places are named after other towns: Moscow, ID, on "An Exotic Map," was named by the town's first postmaster who had been born in Moscow, PA, and raised in Moscow, IA. (Before this, the town was called Paradise, having evolved directly from its original name: Hogs Heaven.) Some towns are named after an aspect of the local environment, like the animals, plants, trees, or climate—but it's easy to be misled. For example, Snowflake, AZ, on "A Weathered Map," is named after two settlers, Snow and Flake.

There are humorous origins, as in the case of Searchlight, NV, also on "An Eccentric Map," which got its name as the result of a discussion about mining in the area. A local suggested it might be possible to strike gold, but they'd need a searchlight to find it. Sometimes in the United States, the humor lies just below the surface, as in the community of Mountain, WV, on "An Unimaginative Map." This little town was called Mole Hill until 1949, when local residents felt compelled to make the proverbial change.

When reading this atlas, it is necessary to remember that, in the words of semanticist Alfred Korzybski, "A map is not the territory," in more ways than one. Due to space limitations, not every town relating to a particular theme could fit onto these pages. There are, for instance, dozens of communities named Midway in the United States; Texas alone has fifteen places so designated. It should also be noted that the places featured on these maps range from rural communities to large cities. The smallest places may not appear on a common road map, but would usually be known by people living in the general vicinity.

The states of Alaska and Hawaii are not featured on the maps, either, for two reasons. First, due to the aforementioned space limitations, it would have been awkward to fit them on the page. Second, neither state had many names to contribute to the particular themes in this atlas. To some extent, this is because a fair number of towns in both states are in the language of the indigenous people, making comprehension by non–native speakers more difficult.

I'm aware that the relevance of a few place-names may escape even the most erudite reader. Let me recommend the Webster's Third New International Dictionary or one of equal heft. Any remaining questions may require delving into books that deal with the particular theme in some depth. There is a wonderful story about the comedian W. C. Fields. Early in his career, he put together a vaudeville act that involved amazing feats at a pool table. As a poolhall was then considered to be a low-class locale, it was suggested to Fields that a large part of his audience might be unfamiliar with various references he was making. "We must strive to educate and uplift as well as entertain," he replied.

I have always loved maps. And in creating this atlas I have had a lot of fun with them. There is an amazingly pleasurable feeling that can come from creating a map of a world that is just the way one wants it to be. I hope that this atlas will help to make geography more enjoyable. It is a subject too important to ignore because, as any mapmaker would tell you, "Without geography you're nowhere." ❧❧❧

David Jouris
Berkeley, Calif.
Spring 1994

This is the short and the long of it.
—WILLIAM SHAKESPEARE

The following postal zip code abbreviations for the fifty states are used in this atlas:

AK	Alaska	LA	Louisiana	OH	Ohio
AL	Alabama	MA	Massachusetts	OK	Oklahoma
AR	Arkansas	MD	Maryland	OR	Oregon
AZ	Arizona	ME	Maine	PA	Pennsylvania
CA	California	MI	Michigan	RI	Rhode Island
CO	Colorado	MN	Minnesota	SC	South Carolina
CT	Connecticut	MO	Missouri	SD	South Dakota
DE	Delaware	MS	Mississippi	TN	Tennessee
FL	Florida	MT	Montana	TX	Texas
GA	Georgia	NB	Nebraska	UT	Utah
HI	Hawaii	NC	North Carolina	VT	Vermont
IA	Iowa	ND	North Dakota	VA	Virginia
ID	Idaho	NH	New Hampshire	WA	Washington
IL	Illinois	NJ	New Jersey	WI	Wisconsin
IN	Indiana	NM	New Mexico	WV	West Virginia
KS	Kansas	NV	Nevada	WY	Wyoming
KY	Kentucky	NY	New York		

In these fifty states, the town with the lowest zip code number, 01001, is Agawam, MA, a town near the Connecticut River in the southwestern part of the state. *Agawam* is an Algonquian word meaning "lowland." The highest zip code number issued so far, 99929, is held by Wrangell, AK. The town is named after Baron Ferdinand von Wrangell, who served as governor of Russian America. Yes, there really was a *Russian* America. This was during the first half of the 1800s, when Alaska was a Russian colony.

And, just for the record, the zip of Zap, ND, is 58580.

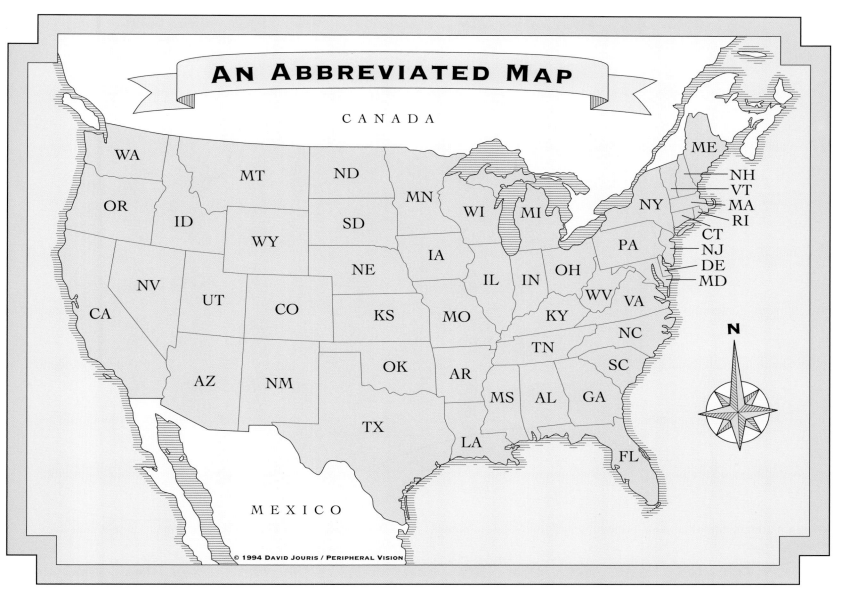

AN ABBREVIATED MAP

CANADA

WA
MT
ND
MN
ME
NH
VT
MA
RI
OR
ID
WY
SD
WI
MI
NY
CT
NJ
DE
MD
NV
UT
CO
NE
IA
IL
IN
OH
PA
CA
KS
MO
KY
WV
VA
AZ
NM
OK
AR
TN
NC
SC
MS
AL
GA
TX
LA
FL

MEXICO

N

© 1994 DAVID JOURIS / PERIPHERAL VISION

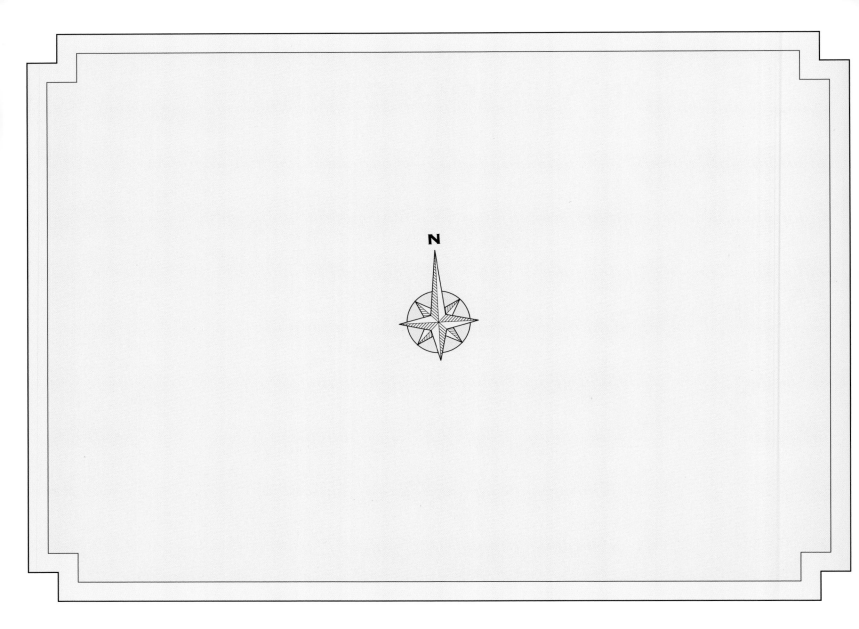

ARTISTIC MAPS

Improvisations on a Theme

A classic is something that everybody wants
to have read and nobody wants to read.
—MARK TWAIN

I don't know which is more discouraging,
literature or chickens.
—E. B. WHITE

There are several stories of how **Dante, SD**, got its name. The most likely version is that the owner of the townsite named it for a favorite author. It should be noted that some residents believe the name was chosen because of the association of Dante with Hell. Sounds like a lovely place.

Twain, CA, is located in an area where Mark Twain once had some mining claims. The town was named by Calvin Higbie, a mining partner and friend, a few months after the author's death in 1910. Forty years earlier, Twain dedicated his book *Roughing It* to Higbie, "an honest man, a genial comrade, and a steadfast friend . . . in memory of the curious time when we two were millionaires for ten days."

Pippa Passes, KY, named for a poem by Robert Browning, is the home of Alice Lloyd College. In the early 1900s, the founder of the college solicited funds from the Robert Browning Societies of New England and subsequently named the home of her new college in honor of Browning's poem. The poem, *Pippa Passes*, is best known for its line: "God's in His heaven—All's right with the world!"

The novel *Ben Hur*, one of the most popular books of the nineteenth century, inspired the names of several places in the United States. **Ben Hur, CA**, took the name during the late 1800s, during the height of the book's success; **Ben Hur, VA**, was so named by a friend of Lew Wallace, the book's author. Wallace was a rather interesting fellow. In addition to writing a number of novels, he was a major general in the Union army during the Civil War, the governor of New Mexico Territory (during which time he wrote *Ben Hur*), and ambassador to Turkey.

The community of **Frankenstein, MO**, appears to have taken its name from an early settler of German extraction named Franken, and not from Mary Shelley's classic gothic novel. The ending *-stein* (meaning "stone" in German) was added as a reference to the area's rocky terrain.

Tarzan, TX, honors the fictional character who lived among the apes. And let's not overlook Tarzana, CA. That's where Edgar Rice Burroughs lived when he wrote those great jungle adventures.

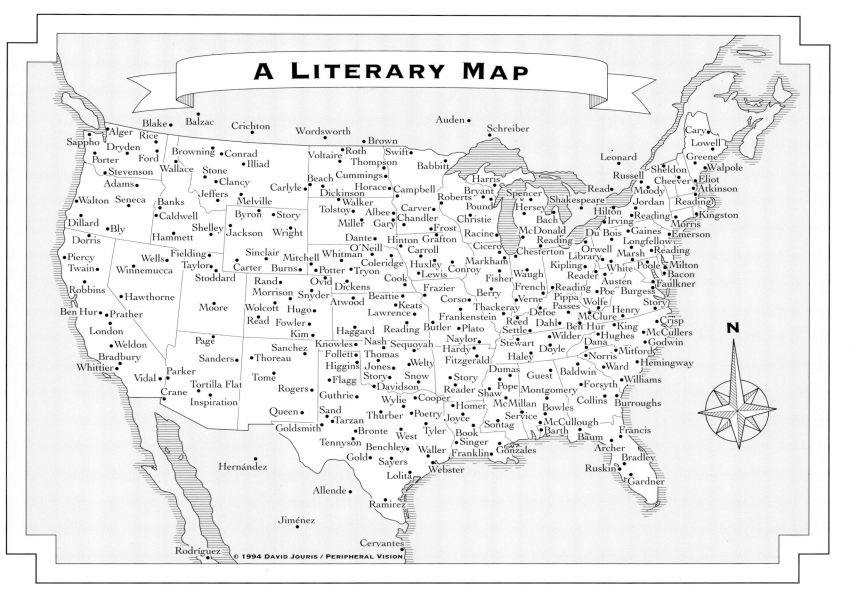

A LITERARY MAP

© 1994 David Jouris / Peripheral Vision

15

The cinema is not a slice of life but a piece of cake.
—**Alfred Hitchcock**

It's a little bit like watching your ox being turned into a bouillon cube.
—**John Le Carré**, *on how it felt seeing one of his books being made into a film*

Gene Autry, OK, was dubbed for the cowboy singer and actor. In November 1941, the cowboy star bought a large ranch near the town, and residents held a huge celebration in his honor. Autry's plan to invest a lot of money in his new ranch—to make it the headquarters for the biggest rodeo show ever—was interrupted by the American entry into WWII. Autry dropped his plans, joined the Army Air Corps, and later sold the ranch.

Fonda, NY, was originally an American Indian community. In the mid-1700s, it saw the arrival of the Dutch and, in 1851, was named for one of the original Dutch founders. It is from this same family that several generations of well-known actors have come.

The settlement of **Bankhead, AL**, was named for Senator John Hollis Bankhead, who lived a few miles away. The good Senator is perhaps more widely known for his progeny. His son William was the Speaker of the House of Representatives and served in Congress for more than twenty years. One of his granddaughters was the actress Tallulah Bankhead, known for her film roles in the 1930s and '40s, as well as for her razor-sharp tongue. She acknowledged her uniqueness, commenting, "Nobody can be exactly like me. Sometimes even I have trouble doing it." The actress was, herself, named for another place—Tallulah Falls, GA—via her grandmother, who was named Tallulah because she was conceived there.

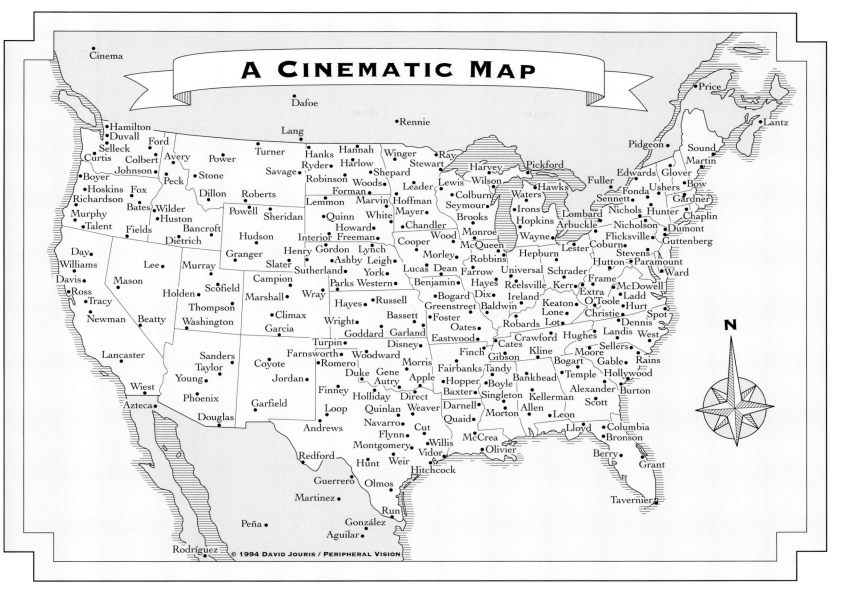

A CINEMATIC MAP

© 1994 DAVID JOURIS / PERIPHERAL VISION

> There is no part of the world where nomenclature is so rich, poetical,
> humorous, and picturesque as the United States of America. All times,
> races and languages have brought their contribution. . . . There are few
> poems with a nobler music for the ear: a songful, tuneful land.
> **—ROBERT LOUIS STEVENSON**

Originally a park, **Mozart, WV**, was founded in the 1890s by brewer Henry Schmulbach as a place for people from the city of Wheeling to have fun—and drink his beer. In those days, Wheeling was home to a large number of singing societies, and many concerts took place in the park presenting music by Mozart, Beethoven, and other well-known composers. These days, only a small part of the original park remains; the rest has become a residential area—perhaps only music to the ears of real estate agents. (The names of Mozart's streets are unrelated to the famous composer; one wishes that some inspired naming would have produced A Major Street, B Flat Major Street, C Minor Street, etc.)

The small town of **Organ, NM**, takes its name from the nearby Organ Mountains. The mountains themselves got their name from rock formations that resemble the pipes of a pipe organ. It was on the road out of Organ that sheriff Pat Garrett, best known for having ended the career of Billy the Kid, was shot to death in 1908.

Fiddletown, CA, began as a mining camp during California's Gold Rush in the mid 1800s. It seems there were a number of fiddle-players among the miners living there, hence the name. One can still hear fiddling in Fiddletown most weekends. **Fiddlesticks, FL**, however, was not named in reference to the bow used in playing the fiddle, but because the developers of this country-club community were looking for a one-word name that was memorable and had some connection to golf. (The reference being that golf clubs are also termed "sticks.")

The rural community named **Ding Dong, TX**, began when two cousins named Bell opened a store there. A local who was hired to paint the store's sign designed a pictorial pun with a bell on each end of the sign with the words "Ding Dong" in between. By the way, Ding Dong is located in Bell County.

Ladora, IA, was named by a music teacher. She derived it from the *la*, *do*, and *re* in the musical scale, with a little poetic license. Apparently, the teacher felt that these assembled tones struck just the right chord for her town's name.

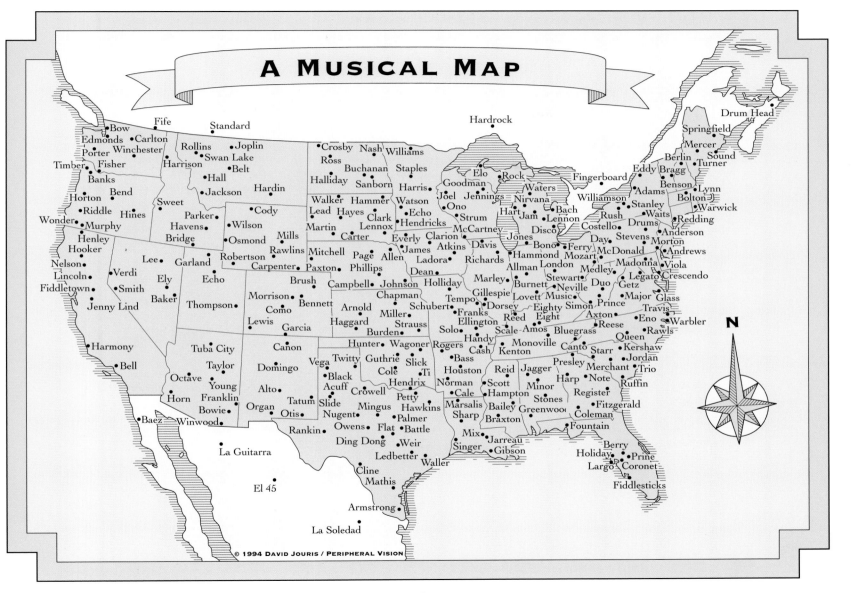

A MUSICAL MAP

Art teaches nothing, except the significance of life.
—**Henry Miller**

Art is art. Everything else is everything else.
—**Ad Reinhardt**

Founded by artists and writers in the early 1900s, **Beaux Arts, WA**, began as a fifty-acre colony on Lake Washington. It was hoped that the community would become a place where artists and craftspeople would live and work in harmony with nature. By the mid 1920s, however, the artists' colony began to dissolve due to the fact that it was art-lovers, rather than art-creators, who could afford to live there. Beaux Arts is now a residential community—although its bungalows, rustic setting, and narrow, curbless streets make it quite different from its suburban neighbors.

The little community of **Cerulean, KY**, got its start as a health resort named Cerulean Springs in the early 1800s. People from far and wide came to this spa for the water, which reportedly has curative properties. The town's colorful name came about in 1811, when, according to local legend, an earthquake changed the springs' black sulfur content to a sky-blue chloride of magnesia.

The town of **Hazel Green, WI**, was probably christened after the like-named town in Kentucky. (The Kentucky town was named by the first settlers who arrived there in the autumn. Apparently all the foliage had changed color except the hazel-nut bushes, which were still green.) The other theory is that the name came about because of the abundance of hazel brush in the Wisconsin locale. Prior to becoming Hazel Green, this Wisconsin town was called Hard Scrabble, for the land yielded a meager living only with great difficulty.

In its early days, **Ebony, VA**, had a general store, a school, and a racetrack—all it really needed, some might argue. The community got its name from a prize-winning black racehorse named Ebony.

Ecru, MS, was named after the color of paint on the town train station. With a less imaginative citizenry, might the town have been named Beige?

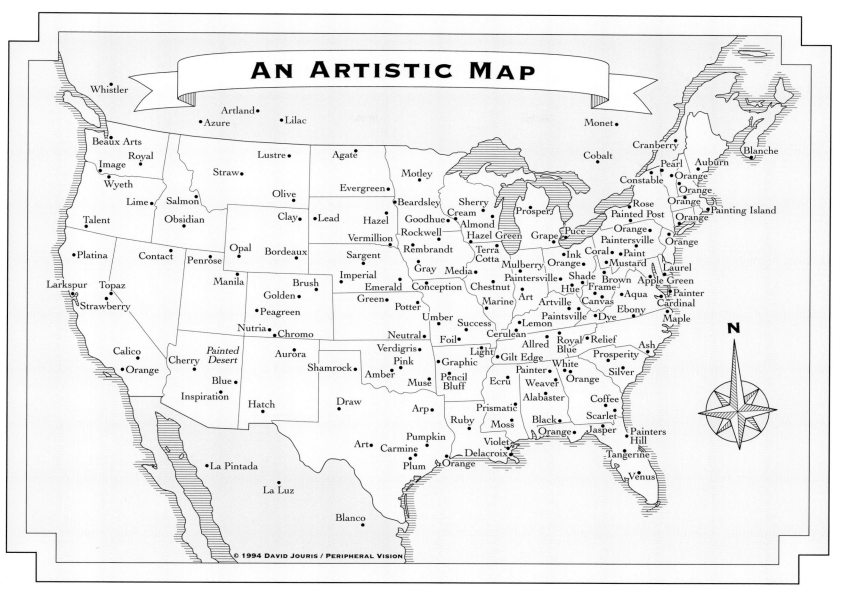

An Artistic Map

Whistler

Artland • •Lilac
Azure •

Monet •

Beaux Arts
Image •Royal
Wyeth •
Lime •
Talent •
Obsidian •
Salmon

Lustre •
Straw •
Olive •
Clay •
•Lead

Agate •
Evergreen •

Motley •

Beardsley •
Goodhue •
Rockwell •
Vermillion
Rembrandt •
Sargent •

Sherry •
Cream •
Almond •
Hazel Green •
Terra
Cotta

Cobalt •

Cranberry •
Pearl •
Auburn •
Constable • Orange •
Orange •
Orange •

Blanche •

Rose •
Painted Post •
Grape • Puce •
Orange •
Ink • Coral •
Mulberry • Orange •
Shade •
Painter •

Painting Island •

Platina •
Contact •
Penrose •
Opal •
Bordeaux

Hazel •
Sargent •
Imperial •
Emerald •
Green •

Gray •
Media •
Conception •
Chestnut •
Marine •
Art •
Artville •

Painter •
Paint •
Orange •
Paintersville •
Mustard •
Brown • Apple Green •
Frame •
Canvas •
Ebony •
Laurel •
Aqua •
Cardinal •
Maple •

Larkspur •
Topaz •
Strawberry •
Manila •
Brush •
Golden •
Peagreen •
Nutria •
Chromo •

Potter •
Umber •
Neutral •
Verdigris •
Success •
Foil •
Cerulean •
Lemon •
Paintsville •
Dye •
Relief •
Allred • Royal
Blue
Prosperity •
Ash •
Silver •

Calico •
Orange •

Painted
Desert
Cherry •
Blue •
Inspiration

Aurora •
Shamrock •
Amber •
Muse •
Hatch •

Pink •
Graphic •
Pencil
Bluff
Light • Gilt Edge •
Painter •
White •
Weaver •
Alabaster •

Ecru •
Orange •

Coffee •
Scarlet •

Draw •
Arp •
Ruby •
Prismatic •
Moss •
Black •
Orange •

Jasper •
Painters
Hill

Art •
Carmine •
Plum •
Pumpkin •
Orange •
Violet •
Delacroix •
Tangerine •
Venus •

La Pintada •

La Luz

Blanco •

N

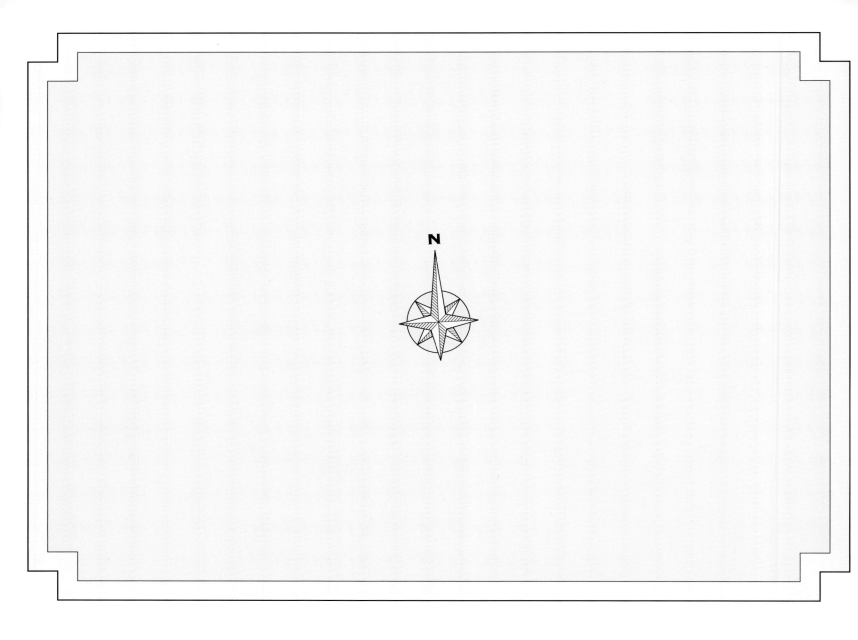

Natural Maps

There Were Plants and Birds and Rocks and Things

All animals are equal, but some are more equal than others.
—GEORGE ORWELL

Why, if a fish came to *me*, and told me he was going on a journey,
I should say, "With what porpoise?"
—LEWIS CARROLL

Dinosaur, CO, is located just south of Dinosaur National Monument. The town boasts several statues of dinosaurs—one of a stegosaurus in front of city hall and two others at the junction of the town's two main highways. Local streets are even named for extinct reptiles, such as Tyrannosaurus Trail and Brontosaurus Boulevard. (Up at the National Monument there are full-size replicas of dinosaur skeletons, as well as a site showing dinosaur bones still embedded in rock.)

Passenger pigeons once roosted in the area that is now **Pigeon, PA**. Eventually hunted to extinction, the birds were once so abundant here that the sky grew dark when the large flocks flew past. John James Audubon once wrote of watching a mile-wide flock of these birds taking more than three hours to pass overhead.

The hamlet of **Hippo, KY**, was named for a local resident, the husband of the woman who ran the first post office there. Because he complained all the time, the man was called "Hippo"—once a not uncommon Southern nickname for a hypochondriac.

Titonka, IA, takes its name from the Sioux word for buffalo—literally, "big black." At one time there were significant numbers of buffalo in this region, and, after one big hunt in the 1850s, the daughter of a white settler gave the town its name.

Salmon, ID, is named for the fish in the Salmon River that flows nearby. Of course, being the longest river in Idaho, the Salmon River runs by a lot of places.

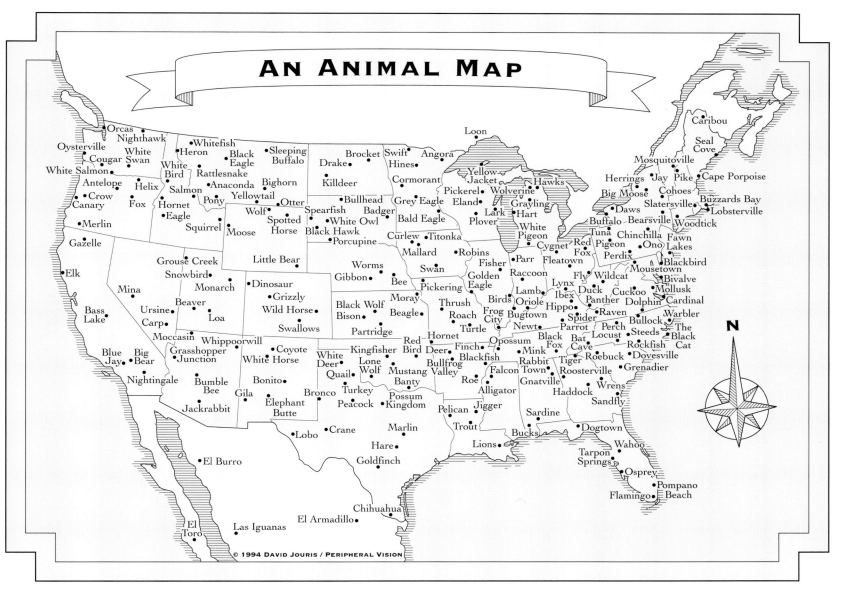

AN ANIMAL MAP

Say it with flowers.
—**P. F. O'KEEFE**,
slogan of the Society of American Florists

Rose is a rose is a rose is a rose.
—**GERTRUDE STEIN**

A number of places with floral names have taken their names from plants that grow in the vicinity. **Azalea, OR**, was named for these colorful flowering bushes, which are abundant in the region. The town was once named Starvout, which is just as colorful in its own way.

The name of **Ajo, AZ**, represents a mixture of cultures and languages. The Papago tribe called the place *Au'auho*, meaning "paint," because of the red copper ore that was found there and used for body paint. When Mexican miners arrived, they mispronounced the word so that it sounded very much like *ajo*, a Spanish word meaning "lily." The name caught on because of the profusion of wild lilies in the area.

The first settlers in the region around **Wild Rose, WI**, came from Rose, NY, in the mid 1800s and named their new township Rose. The village was named Wild Rose to distinguish it from the township, and also because of the wild roses in the area.

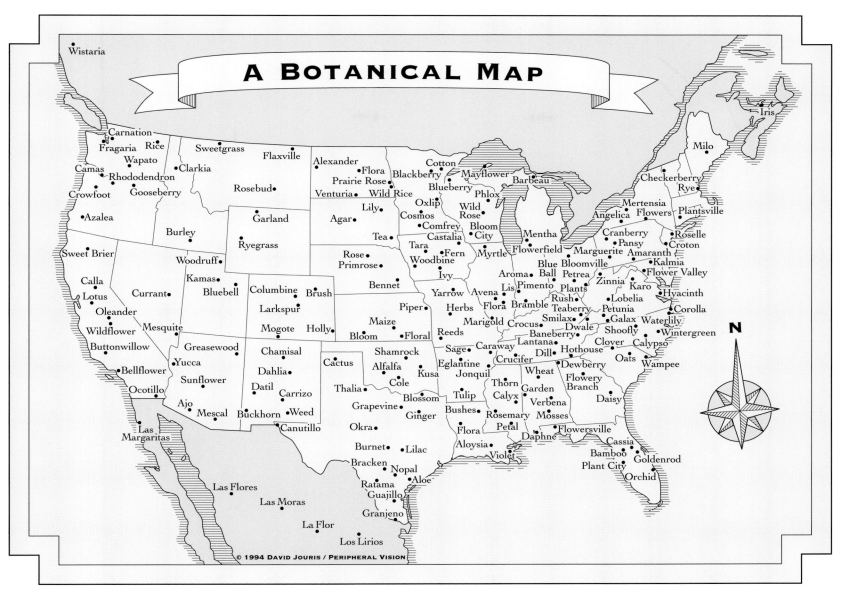

A BOTANICAL MAP

Wistaria

Iris

Carnation
Fragaria Rice
Wapato
Camas
Rhododendron
Crowfoot Gooseberry
Azalea

Sweetgrass
Flaxville
Rosebud

Alexander
Flora Blackberry
Prairie Rose
Venturia Wild Rice
Oxlip
Cosmos

Cotton
Mayflower Barbeau
Blueberry Phlox
Wild
Rose

Milo

Checkerberry
Rye
Mertensia
Angelica Flowers Plantsville

Burley

Garland
Ryegrass

Lily
Agar
Tea

Comfrey Bloom
Castalia City
Tara
Woodbine Fern Myrtle
Ivy

Mentha
Flowerfield
Blue Bloomville
Aroma Ball Petrea

Cranberry
Pansy
Marguerite Amaranth
Kalmia
Flower Valley

Roselle
Croton

Sweet Brier

Woodruff

Rose
Primrose

Bennet

Lis
Yarrow Pimento Plants
Avena Flora Teaberry
Herbs Bramble Rush
Marigold Crocus
Smilax
Baneberry
Lantana

Zinnia
Karo
Lobelia
Petunia Galax
Dwale Shoofly
Clover
Hothouse

Corolla
Hyacinth

Waterlily
Wintergreen
Calypso

Calla
Lotus
Oleander
Wildflower
Buttonwillow

Kamas
Currant Bluebell

Columbine Brush
Larkspur
Mogote Holly

Piper

Maize
Bloom Floral

Sage
Eglantine
Jonquil

Reeds

Caraway
Crucifer Dill

Oats
Wampee

Greasewood
Yucca
Sunflower
Ojo

Chamisal
Dahlia
Datil Carrizo

Cactus

Shamrock
Alfalfa
Kusa
Cole

Thorn
Wheat Garden
Calyx Verbena

Dewberry
Flowery
Branch

Daisy

Mesquite

Bellflower
Ocotillo

Mescal Buckhorn Weed
Canutillo

Thalia
Grapevine
Okra

Blossom Tulip
Ginger Bushes
Flora

Rosemary Mosses
Petal

Flowersville

Daphne

Cassia
Bamboo

Las
Margaritas

Burnet Lilac
Bracken
Nopal
Ratama Aloe
Guajillo
Granjeno

Aloysia
Violet

Plant City

Goldenrod
Orchid

Las Flores
Las Moras
La Flor
Los Lirios

N

© 1994 David Jouris / Peripheral Vision

> The meek shall inherit the earth—
> but not the mineral rights.
> —ATTRIBUTED TO **J. PAUL GETTY**

Pipestone, MN, is named for a nearby quarry of red pipestone, or catlinite, long prized by Native Americans, who have found this soft stone useful for carving into tobacco pipes. In former times, tobacco was found over much of the area that has become the United States, but pipestone was not nearly as common and thus proved quite valuable for trading. Pipestone is frequently found in local nomenclature, not only as the name of the town, but also the county and the National Monument in this small corner of southwestern Minnesota.

Fifty percent of the world's sapphires come from Montana. And right in the heart of the state is **Sapphire Village, MT**, site of the Yogo sapphire mine. Yogo sapphires range in color from cornflower blue to purple and are known for their clarity.

Leadville, CO, first gained fame as a gold-mining town in 1860 and later became Colorado's silver capital. During its history, the area around Leadville has also yielded zinc, manganese, molybdenum, and, of course, lead. The town of **Lead, SD**, has the largest gold-producing mine in the Western Hemisphere. One might wonder why a town that is famous for gold would be named Lead. It turns out that the town isn't named after the mineral, or pronounced that way (it rhymes with "deed"). In mining, a leading vein or "lead," is an ore vein that indicates that a mineral deposit may be present.

Boron, CA, was named for the element in borax. When a large mining company moved to the community to mine the borax deposits found in the area, the name was changed from Amargo to Boron. *Amargo* is the Spanish word for "bitter," which was how the borax made the water taste.

The element boron, by the way, has made a huge impact on the world of gems. It seems that the Hope Diamond's bluish color is due to a trace amount of boron. **Blue Diamond, NV**, isn't named for a gem, however, but for a brand of gypsum board, or sheetrock. The Blue Diamond company mined gypsum from a mountain here; as the company basically owned the town in the early days, the name seemed logical. The gypsum board company is still going strong, albeit under another name. The citizens decided to keep the name Blue Diamond alive, however, realizing it had a bit more allure than did the town's former name of Cottonwood.

Magnet, TX, was named in the hope that its appellation would "attract" people.

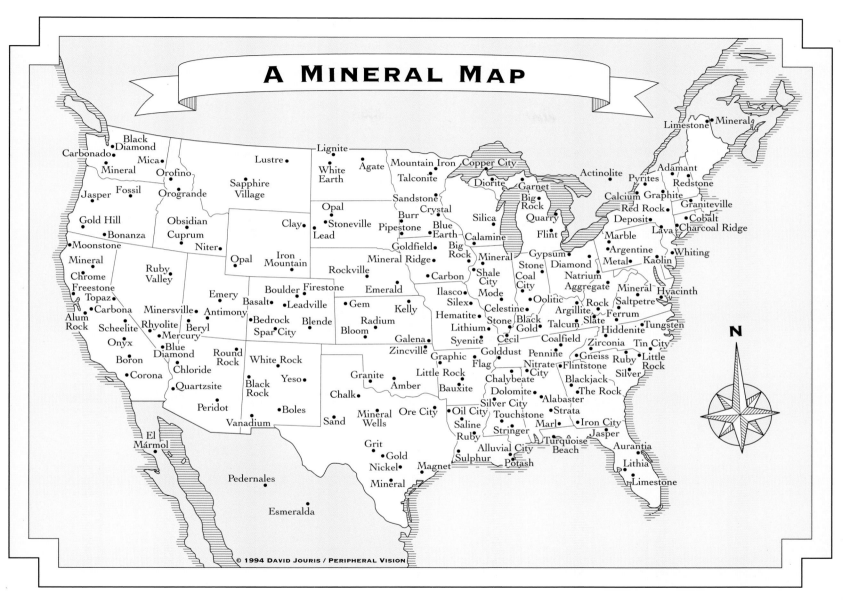

A MINERAL MAP

Astronomy compels the soul to look upwards and leads
us from this world to another.
—**PLATO**

Astrology is astronomy brought to earth and applied.
—**RALPH WALDO EMERSON**

Most people seem to agree that the town of **Mars, PA**, was named after a man named Marshall who helped construct a house for the man who served as first postmaster and who was instrumental in getting a post office assigned to the town. The only hint of disagreement comes from an old plaque stating that the town was named after the planet. Anybody can put up a plaque, of course, but this plaque was put up on what was then the historical society building.

Jupiter, FL, was one of a number of Florida communities (including places like Mars and Venus) known collectively as the Galaxy. The little railroad that connected these places was popularly called the Celestial Railroad.

Sunrise, FL, is an example of bucking the natural order of going from Sunrise to Sunset. The town was originally named Sunset and was planned as a retirement community. The developers found out pretty quickly that retirees don't like to be reminded that they are in the "sunset" of their lives, so a more optimistic name was chosen.

Its first postmaster gave **Earth, TX**, its name. The man said it was so barren there, without a tree in sight, that "all you could see was earth."

Curiously, **Sun Valley, ID**, is located about fifty miles northwest of Craters of the Moon National Monument. Craters of the Moon, by the way, is sometimes mentioned as having been used by NASA as a location for training astronauts. This could be true only if one accepts that public relations tours are an integral part of training.

Aurora, NC, was formerly a settlement named Betty Town, inhabited by freed black slaves. It was changed to Aurora in honor of the *Aurora Borealis*—not the atmospheric phenomenon, but an erstwhile county newspaper of that name.

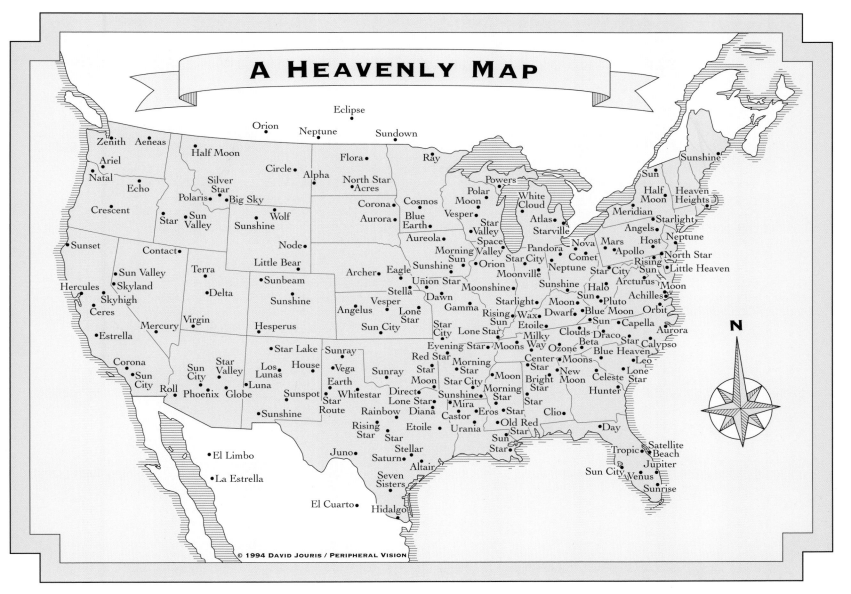

A HEAVENLY MAP

Eclipse

Orion Neptune Sundown

Zenith Aeneas Half Moon Flora Ray Sunshine

Ariel Circle Alpha North Star Sun

Natal Silver Acres Powers Half Heaven

Echo Star Corona Cosmos Polar White Moon Heights

Crescent Polaris Big Sky Aurora Blue Moon Cloud Meridian

Star Sun Wolf Earth Vesper Atlas Starlight

Valley Sunshine Star Starville Angels

Node Valley Space Host Neptune

Sunset Contact Little Bear Aureola Pandora Nova Mars

Morning Star City Comet Apollo North Star

Sun Valley Terra Sun Orion Neptune Star City Rising

Hercules Skyland Sunbeam Archer Eagle Sunshine Moonville Sun Little Heaven

Skyhigh Delta Union Star Moonshine Arcturus Moon

Ceres Sunshine Stella Dawn Sun Halo Pluto Achilles Orbit

Mercury Virgin Hesperus Vesper Gamma Starlight Moon Blue Moon Sun Capella

Estrella Angelus Lone Rising Wax Dwarf Clouds Draco Star Aurora

Sun City Star Sun Etoile Beta Calypso

Corona Star Lake Sunray Star Lone Star Milky Ozone Blue Heaven Leo

Sun Star Valley House Vega Evening Star Moons Way Moons Lone

City Los Sunray Red Star Morning Center New Celeste Star

Phoenix Globe Lunas Earth Star Star Moon Bright Moon Hunter

Roll Luna Sunspot Whitestar Direct Sunshine Morning Star

Sunshine Star Lone Star Diana Mira Star Clio

Route Rainbow Castor Eros Star

Rising Etoile Urania Old Red Day

El Limbo Star Star Sun Satellite

Juno Star Star Tropic Beach

La Estrella Stellar Jupiter

Saturn Sun City Venus

El Cuarto Hidalgo Seven Altair Sunrise

Sisters

N

Everybody talks about the weather, but
nobody does anything about it.
—**MARK TWAIN**

When God sorts out the weather and sends
rain … rain's my choice.
—**JAMES WHITCOMB RILEY**

The town now known as **Frostproof, FL**, began with the name Keystone City. The Post Office Department asked the residents to find a new name to avoid confusion with a town in the northern part of the state named Keystone Heights. Some years later, in the late 1800s, two severe freezes hit Florida, destroying the citrus crop and most of the trees. Although the freeze did hit the area, the citrus trees didn't sustain much damage, probably due to the town's location in a hilly area between two lakes. Residents quickly realized that Frostproof was the name they'd been looking for. Although some people might jump to the conclusion that a town with a name like this wouldn't have *any* frost, the citizens who chose the name were apparently sticklers for accuracy: they did not name it *Frostfree*.

Butterfly, KY, is said to have gotten its name because of the large number of butterflies observed there. One of the most amazing hypotheses in the realm of weather forecasting is what is known as the butterfly effect. Relying on the mathematical theory of chaos, the hypothesis holds that the motion of a butterfly's wings today somewhere in, let's say, Kentucky, causes a rippling through the atmosphere that can have a dramatic effect a month later on the weather on the other side of the world.

Goose pimples, also called gooseflesh or goose bumps, are usually brought about by cold or fear. In the case of **Goose Pimple Junction, VA**, it turns out to be the latter. One of the early residents here in the 1800s built a new house and rented out his former home to a couple newly arrived in the area. It soon became obvious that the new man beat his wife; when the landlord heard the screaming, goose pimples rose on his skin. In time, as neighbors heard the landlord's description, the nearby junction acquired its ill-gotten name.

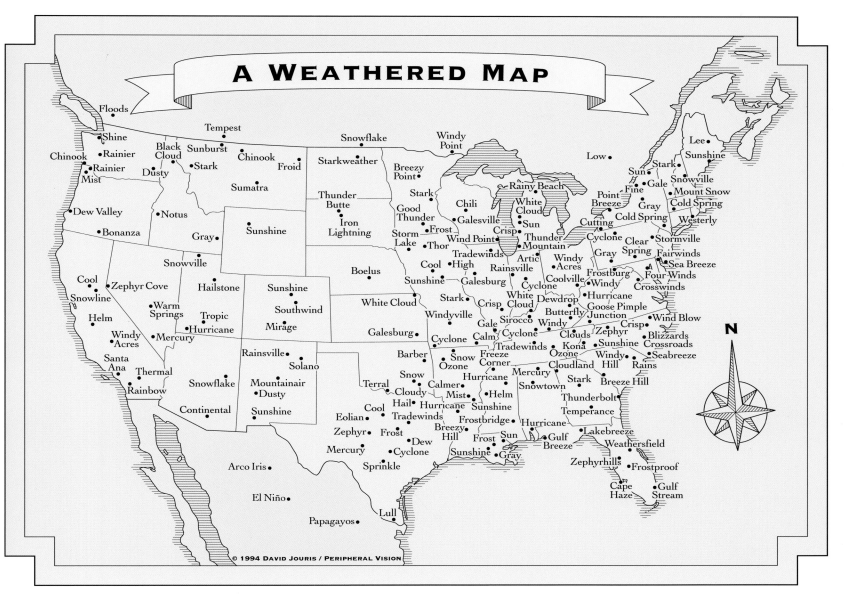

A WEATHERED MAP

© 1994 David Jouris / Peripheral Vision

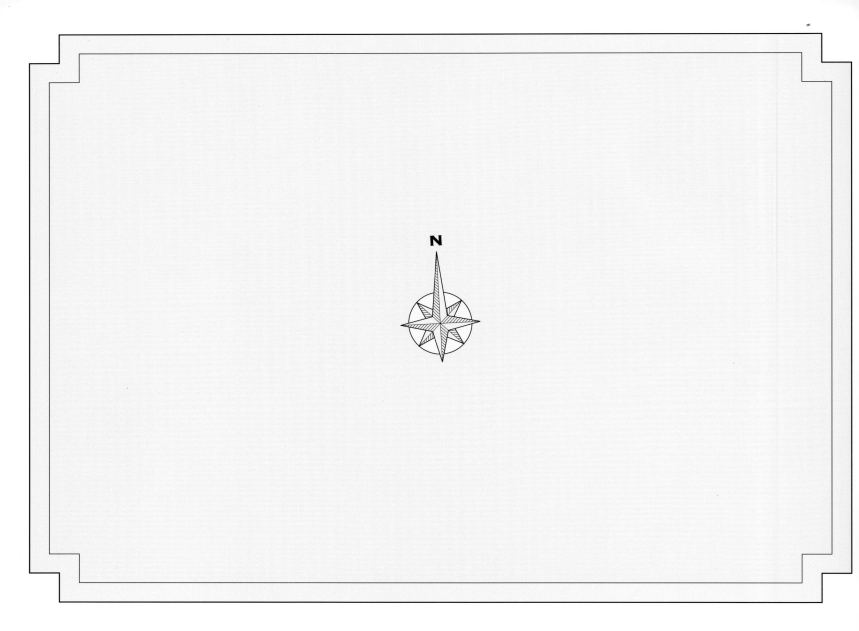

Divine Maps

On a Mission from God—and Goddess

Mythology: the body of a primitive people's beliefs
concerning its origin, early history, heroes,
deities and so forth, as distinguished from the
true accounts which it invents later.
—AMBROSE BIERCE

It is not down in any map; true places never are.
—HERMAN MELVILLE

Phoenix, AZ, is located on the ruins of a Native American town. One of the founders of the new town suggested the name Phoenix because the settlers were raising a new city on the ashes of an old one, similar to the way the mythical phoenix rose from its own ashes. Given the temperature in Phoenix during the summer, the name is also reminiscent of the heat created when the mythical bird flapped its wings and fanned the flames.

Hercules, CA, got its name from the Hercules Powder Company, which was in business there. The company first used the name Hercules to suggest that its explosive black powder was as powerful as the mythological hero. To help give the black powder a "kick," a rosin was used in the charge. Through a fascinating series of events involving General Santa Ana (Davy Crockett's nemesis at the Alamo), a soap and baking powder manufacturer named Wrigley, and World War II, the Hercules Powder Company diversified to become the world's largest supplier of rosin—used, among other things, as a binder in chewing gum. It seems ironic that a company that makes products to blow things apart is also involved in making a product to hold things together.

Originally, the town of **Clio, MI**, was named Varna, after a local resident. Some years later, a ladies' club suggested it would be preferable to give the town a name with a more intellectual quality. They proposed Clio, after the Greek muse of history. The hoped-for intellectual heights may not have been attained, however, since there is a widely told tale that suggests the town got its name from the marking on a railroad watering tank, CL-10, that was read as CLIO.

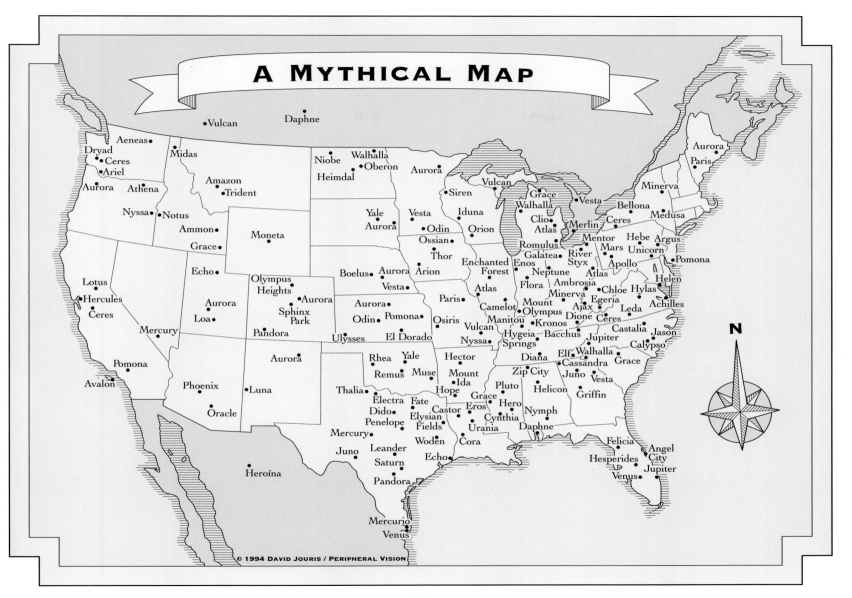

A MYTHICAL MAP

© 1994 David Jouris / Peripheral Vision

37

Uz, KY, was named for the biblical land of Uz. Back in the early part of the 1900s, when railroad officials were trying to deal with local landowners in order to build a railroad line, they ran into many difficulties. Two railroad employees were commiserating after a particularly frustrating day, and one of them said that the trouble they were encountering seemed not unlike the trouble Job had experienced in Uz. From this came the name of the local train station, and eventually the town.

The name of **Nicodemus, KS**, doesn't come from the man who is credited in the Bible with helping to bury Jesus, but from a like-named slave on the second ship that brought African slaves to this country. Legend says that Nicodemus became the first African slave to buy his freedom. The community of Nicodemus, located on the Solomon River, was one of a number of towns that were settled in the 1870s by black homesteaders during the exodus of recently freed slaves from the South after the Civil War. Promotional circulars distributed at the time referred to the "Promised Land" of Kansas. Nicodemus is still an all–African-American town, peopled by the descendants of the original settlers—the only one of the original all-black communities still in existence.

The rural community of **Ai, AL**, takes its name from the Bible, although the reasons for this choice are unknown. The ancient city of Ai, destroyed by Joshua on orders from you-know-Who, was rather prophetically named since, in Hebrew, *Ai* means "heap" or "ruin." It is not quite clear why the ancient city was laid to ruin, but one imagines that the inhabitants had been guilty of a number of the Seven Deadly Sins, including sloth. These days, there isn't much left of Ai, AL, either.

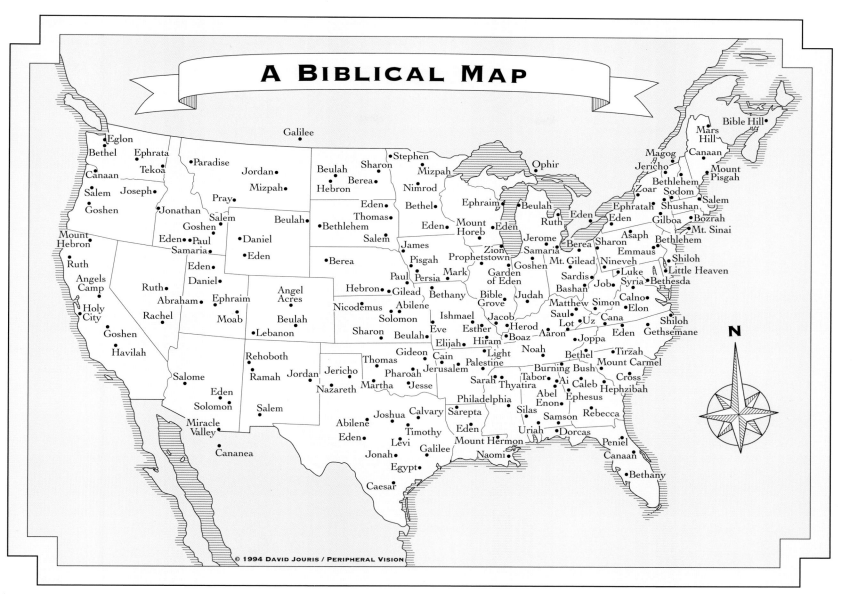

A BIBLICAL MAP

© 1994 David Jouris / Peripheral Vision

Saint: a dead sinner, revised and edited.
—AMBROSE BIERCE

There is a dearth of towns bearing saints' names in New England—in fact, only a handful exist in Maine and Vermont, and none elsewhere. Saints' names weren't used in colonial New England; to the Puritan mind, they smacked too much of papistry. It wasn't until late in the eighteenth century that a couple of saints' names crept in. **St. Albans, VT**, was named after the English town of St. Albans, which is often considered the birthplace of human rights because the first draft of the Magna Carta was written there in 1213. Although the early New England colonists would not have knowingly used a saint's name, they seem to have overlooked the origins of the name Boston. The name came from an English town of the same name, but that town's name derived from an Anglo-Saxon word meaning Botulf's Stone, to indicate that it was a place where Botulf, who later gained sainthood, built an abbey and preached.

The only place in the world named **St. Johnsbury** is in Vermont. The town was named by the Revolutionary War hero Ethan Allen for a French nobleman—a farmer, writer, and diplomat based in New York, named Michel-Guillaume St. Jean de Crèvecoeur, whose pen name was J. Hector St. John. Although not actually a saint, the French nobleman humbly suggested to Allen that, as there were already a number of St. Johns in existence, perhaps the name of the town could be slightly altered to St. Johnsbury. (The suffix *-bury* comes from the Old English, meaning "an enclosed or fortified place." Its descendant exists in present-day English as "borough.")

St. Jacob, IL, wasn't named for a saint, either. What eventually became the town was founded on land owned originally by Jacob Schutz, a farmer who, as a sideline, sold whiskey by the gallon. In the mid 1800s, a fellow named Jacob Schroth bought some land on one corner of Schutz's property where he, too, proceeded to go into the business of selling liquor by setting up a saloon and store. This duo was soon joined by a blacksmith named Jacob Willi, and the three of them realized that the community could honor all of them at once by using the name Jacob. They must have had their imaginations working overtime to justify adding the word "Saint."

Originally, the town of **St. Thomas, PA**, was named Campbellstown after its founder, Thomas Campbell. To qualify for a post office a few years later, the town had to change its name to avoid conflict with a like-named community. To maintain the honor paid to Thomas Campbell in the original town name, the residents considered naming the town Thomas. Then, taking into account the character of Campbell, who was a bit of a rascal—and with their tongues firmly in their cheeks—they decided to bestow nominal sainthood on their first citizen at the same time.

The great state of Kansas, testing the patience even of a saintlike geographer, has both a **Saint Marys** and a **St. Marys**.

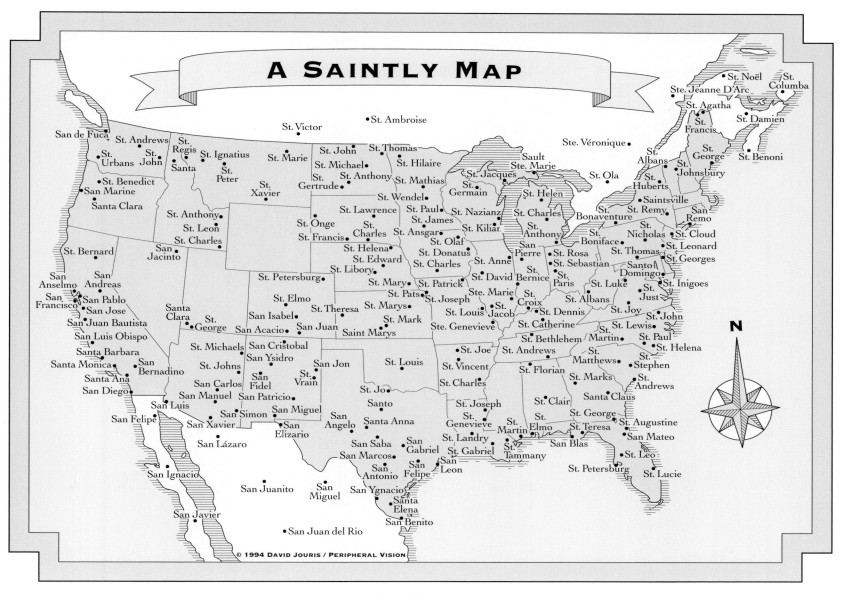

A Saintly Map

St. Noël • • St. Columba
Ste. Jeanne D'Arc •
St. Agatha •
St. Francis • • St. Damien
St. George • • St. Benoni
Ste. Véronique •
St. Albans • St. Benoni
St. Johnsbury •
St. Huberts •
Saintsville •
St. Remy • San Remo •

St. Noël
St. Ambroise •
St. Victor •
St. Andrews
San de Fuca •
St. Urbans • St. • St. Ignatius
St. Regis John
Santa
St. Peter
St. Marie
St. John
St. Michael
St. Thomas
St. Hilaire
St. Anthony
St. Mathias
Sault Ste. Marie
St. Ola
St. Jacques
St. Germain
St. Helen
St. Charles
St. Xavier
St. Gertrude
St. Wendel
St. Lawrence
St. Paul
St. Nazianz
St. Charles
Bonaventure
St. Nicholas
St. Cloud
St. Leonard
St. Anthony
St. Leon
St. Charles
St. Onge
St. Francis
St. Charles
St. Ansgar
St. Kiliar
St. Anthony
St. Boniface
St. Thomas
St. Georges
St. Bernard
San Jacinto
St. Helena
St. Edward
St. Libory
St. Olaf
St. Donatus
St. Charles
San Pierre
St. Rosa
St. Sebastian
Santo Domingo
St. Inigoes
San Anselmo
San Andreas
St. Petersburg.
St. Mary
St. Patrick
St. David
Bernice
Paris
St. Luke
St. Just
San Francisco
San Pablo
San Jose
St. Elmo
St. Theresa
St. Marys
St. Pats
St. Joseph
Ste. Marie
St. Croix
St. Albans
St. Joy
St. John
San Juan Bautista
Santa Clara
St. George
San Acacio
San Juan
St. Mark
St. Louis
St. Jacob
St. Dennis
St. Catherine
St. Lewis
San Luis Obispo
Saint Marys
Ste. Genevieve
St. Bethlehem
Martin
St. Paul
Santa Barbara
St. Michaels
San Cristobal
St. Joe
St. Andrews
St. Matthews
St. Helena
Santa Monica
San Ysidro
San Jon
St. Louis
St. Vincent
St. Florian
St. Stephen
San Bernadino
St. Johns
San Carlos
San Fidel
St. Vrain
St. Charles
St. Marks
St. Andrews
Santa Ana
San Diego
San Manuel
San Patricio
St. Jo
St. Joseph
St. Clair
St. George
Santa Claus
St. Augustine
San Luis
San Simon
San Miguel
Santo
St. Genevieve
St. Martin
St. Elmo
St. Teresa
San Mateo
San Felipe
San Xavier
San Angelo
Santa Anna
St. Landry
St. Gabriel
San Blas
St. Leo
San Elizario
San Saba
San Gabriel
St. Gabriel
St. Tammany
San Lázaro
San Marcos
San Leon
St. Petersburg
St. Lucie
San Ignacio
San Antonio
San Felipe
San Leon
San Juanito
San Miguel
San Ygnacio
Santa Elena
San Javier
San Benito

N

41

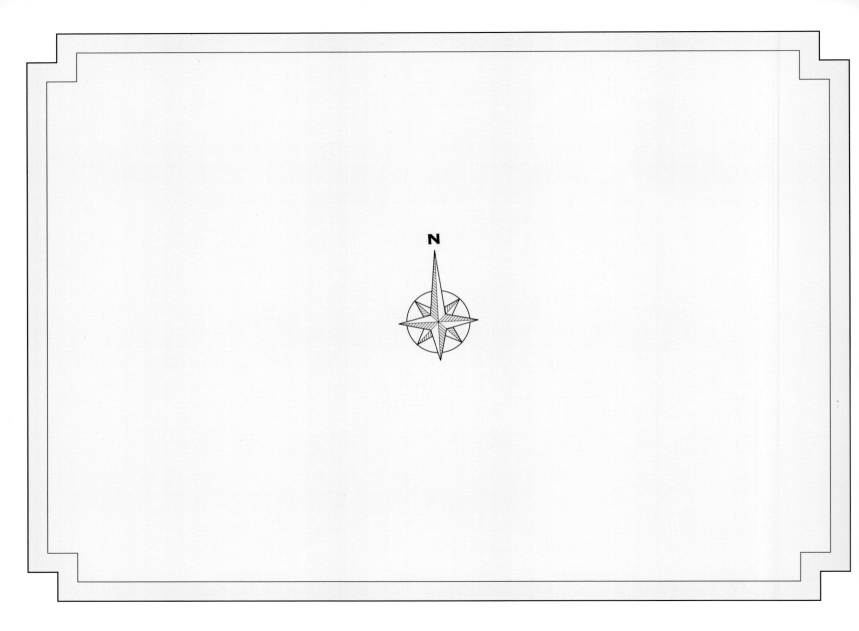

Historical Maps

Geoging Your Memory

> Let ancient times delight other folk; I rejoice that
> I was not born till now; this age suits my nature.
> **—OVID**, CIRCA 13 B.C.

The town of **Leucadia, CA**, is named for one of the Ionian islands in Greece. It is said that in ancient times, the Greek poet Sappho leapt into the sea from one of the island's cliffs after realizing that she was never going to get to first base with her love, Phaon. Curiously, the California town has employed not Greek but Roman names of mythological figures—like Vulcan, Neptune, Diana, and Jupiter—for its streets.

Hinnom, VA, is named for the valley near Jerusalem. The Virginia community seems to have chosen this name because it is likewise located in a valley. One assumes they overlooked Jewish legend that considered the original Hinnom to be the mouth of Hell.

One of the town founders proposed the name of **Rome, GA**, because he noticed the planned town site was located on seven hills, as was the ancient city of Rome.

Dunedin, FL, takes its name from the old Gaelic word for Edinburgh. *Dun* is the word for "town" and *edin* comes from the name of the Irish saint, Edana. The Florida town was originally called Jonesboro, but it was changed in the late 1800s when two Scotsmen came to live there.

The small town of **Utica, MT**, began as a camp used by cowboys in the spring and fall. The first settlers there to experience all four seasons found the bitterly cold Montana winter quite inhospitable and admitted that they had to be crazy to live there year around. They specifically chose the name Utica—not in reference to the ancient Phoenician seaport in North Africa, but because Utica, NY, was the home of the Empire State's lunatic asylum.

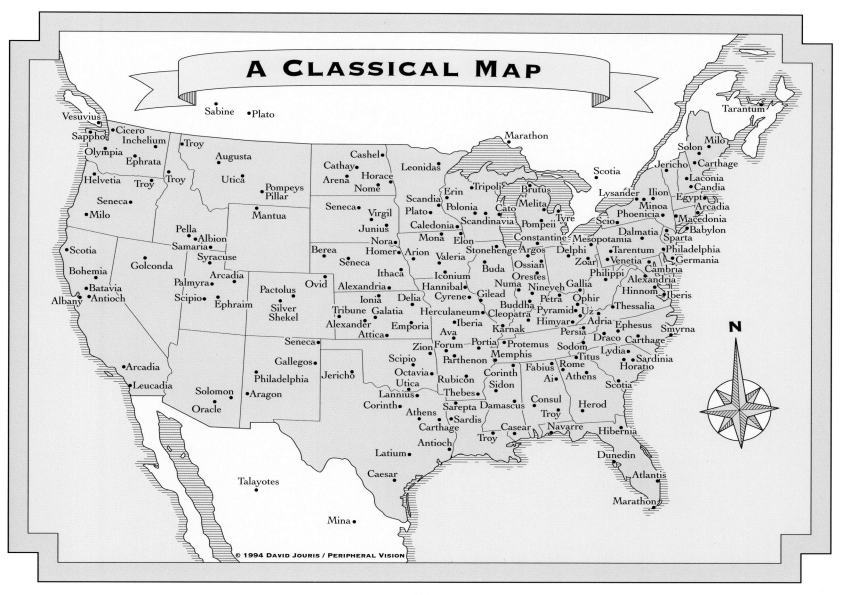

A CLASSICAL MAP

© 1994 David Jouris / Peripheral Vision

45

E pluribus unum.

Quid me anxious sum?

The postal authorities felt the name originally proposed for one Texas town—Cleburne, Johnson Stop—was a mite too long. One resident, not coincidentally named Johnson, insisted that if he and his name were being labeled persona non grata, then the town ought not to be named for anyone. A local school teacher, abiding by that ultimatum, suggested the name **Nemo, TX**—the Latin word for "no one."

Magalia, CA, is the Latin name meaning "huts," a bit of a non sequitur given its previous name, Dogtown. Deciding to alter the status quo only slightly, **Bovina, TX**, went with a more elegant version of its original name, Bull Town.

Taking its name directly from the Latin word meaning "I renew" is **Renovo, PA**. The town is set on a tract of land that was once a location where railroad cars were repaired and renovated.

Altus, OK, once had a different name, as well as a slightly different location. When the town, which was built on low ground, was destroyed in a flood, the residents wisely opted to rebuild the town on safer ground and renamed the town Altus, Latin for "high."

Townfolk believe that **Forsan, TX**, was originally intended to be called Four Sands, after the strata in an oil field, but the name was erroneously transmitted to the Post Office Department as Forsan. This may have been a bona fide mistake, but as some residents were involved in the search for oil, the name Forsan, meaning "perhaps" in Latin, was altogether appropriate.

Arcanum, OH, employs the Latin word for "secret" or "mystery." How the town got its name is a mystery, too.

A lumberman came up with an idea to prevent the repetition of common tree names used in town names. He chose the Latin names for a handful of Missouri towns (e.g., Viburnum—i.e. "honeysuckle," Nyssa—i.e. "sweet gum" or "tupelo," Fagus—i.e. "beech," et cetera). Trivia like this, relating to town names in the United States, is abundant. The word *trivia* itself is Latin for "three roads." Where three roads met, the Romans would often put up notice boards with news on them; the word has come to represent the little bits of information found at these locations, rather than the locations themselves.

A LATIN MAP

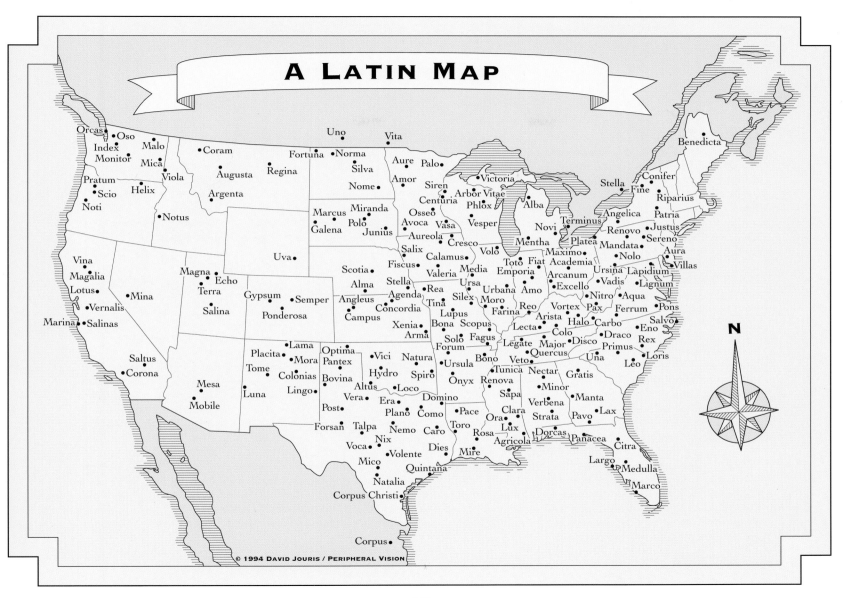

N

47

> They made us many promises, more than I can remember—
> they never kept but one; they promised to take our land,
> and they took it.
> **—RED CLOUD**

In 1830, the Indian Removal Act was signed by notorious Indian fighter and recently elected president Andrew Jackson. This decree called for the forced eviction of all eastern Indians to an area west of the Mississippi River, termed Indian Territory. Although in a subsequent legal battle the Supreme Court found in favor of the Indians, Jackson ignored this decision and ordered the army to begin the evictions. In the southeast, members of the Five Civilized Tribes (Cherokee, Chickasaw, Choctaw, Creek, and Seminole) were moved under appalling conditions. Food, blankets, and wagons were in short supply; disease and bandits also contributed to the demise of more than 25 percent of the Indians en route. Those who survived this Trail of Tears faced equally bitter conditions in the new territory. The names of towns like **Choctaw, MS**, **Cherokee, NC**, **Chickasaw, AL**, and **Seminole, FL**, still serve as faint reminders that huge parts of these states were once home to these Native American peoples.

Near **Cheyenne, OK**, is the Washita Battlefield National Historic Landmark. This was the site of Custer's attack on the sleeping Cheyenne village of Chief Black Kettle in late 1868. The slaughter helped set the stage for Custer's defeat at the Battle of the Little Bighorn in Montana, eight years later.

The Iroquois nation was a democratic confederation of half a dozen Native American tribes, located in what is now New York. Towns like **Mohawk, NY**, **Oneida, NY**, **Onondaga, NY**, and **Cayuga, NY**, bear witness to some of the tribes that formed this Indian nation. Several hundred years before the founding of the United States, the Iroquois had a constitution based on ideals such as freedom of expression and religion, the right to privacy, women's suffrage, checks and balances to prevent abuses of power, a provision to remove leaders who weren't doing their job, and the concept that leaders were the servants of the people. A number of the Founding Fathers of the United States—like Washington, Franklin, and Jefferson—interacted with the Native American tribes and found many democratic principles in action—principles they later incorporated in the Constitution of the United States.

While on the theme of American Indian tribal names, it should be mentioned that the names most commonly used to refer to tribes are not any more accurate than the word "Indian." A few examples: *Dakotas*, meaning "friends" or "allies," is what the Sioux call themselves; *Sioux* is their Chippewa enemies' word for "adder snakes" or "enemies." The Delawares call themselves *Lenape*, meaning "the people"; the name given to them by the white colonists, "Delaware," came from the river along which these indigenous people lived. (The river was named for Lord Thomas West, Baron De La Waar, the colonial governor of Virginia in the early 1600s.)

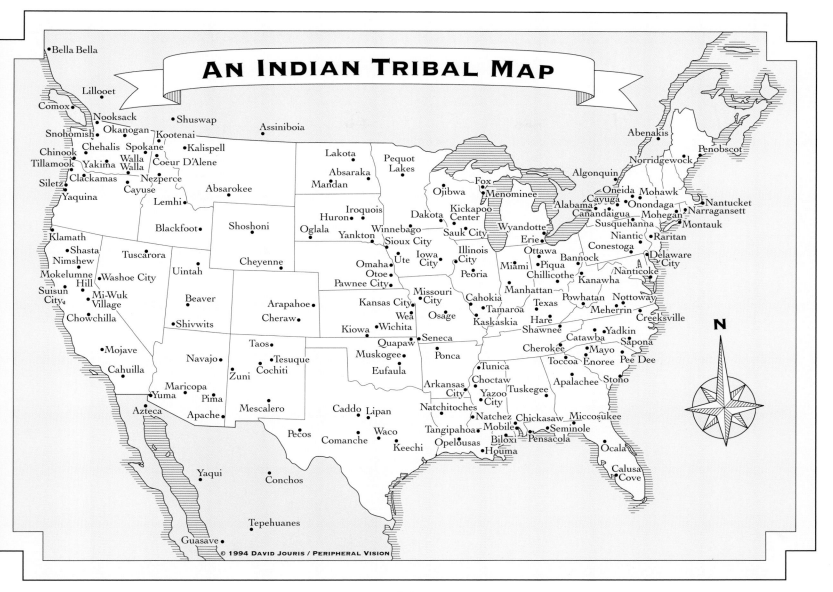

AN INDIAN TRIBAL MAP

• Bella Bella

• Lillooet

Comox •

• Nooksack

Snohomish • Okanogan • Shuswap

• Kootenai • Assiniboia

Chehalis • Spokane • Kalispell

Chinook • Yakima • Walla Walla • Coeur D'Alene

Tillamook • Walla Walla

Siletz • Clackamas • Nezperce

Yaquina • Cayuse

Lemhi •

Absarokee •

Lakota

Absaraka

Mandan

Pequot Lakes

Klamath •

Shasta • Tuscarora

Nimshew •

Mokelumne Hill • Washoe City

Suisun City •

Mi-Wuk Village

Chowchilla •

Mojave •

Cahuilla •

Blackfoot •

Shoshoni

Uintah

Beaver •

Shivwits •

Cheyenne

Arapahoe •

Cheraw •

Taos •

Navajo •

Zuni •

Tesuque •

Cochiti •

Mescalero •

Maricopa •

Yuma •

Azteca •

Pima •

Apache •

Yaqui •

Conchos •

Tepehuanes •

Guasave •

Huron •

Iroquois

Oglala •

Winnebago •

Yankton •

Omaha • Ute

Otoe •

Pawnee City •

Kansas City •

Wea •

Kiowa • Wichita •

Quapaw •

Muskogee •

Eufaula •

Caddo • Lipan •

Waco •

Comanche • Keechi •

Pecos •

Dakota •

Fox

Ojibwa • Menominee

Kickapoo Center

Sioux City •

Sauk City •

Iowa City • Illinois City

Peoria •

Missouri City •

Osage •

Ponca •

Arkansas City •

Natchitoches •

Opelousas •

Tangipahoa •

Wyandotte •

Erie •

Ottawa •

Miami •

Chillicothe •

Manhattan •

Cahokia •

Tamaroa •

Kaskaskia •

Hare •

Shawnee •

Seneca •

Cherokee •

Choctaw •

Yazoo City •

Natchez •

Mobile •

Biloxi •

Houma •

Abenakis •

Algonquin •

Oneida • Mohawk

Cayuga • Onondaga

Alabama • Canandaigua • Mohegan

Susquehanna •

Piqua •

Bannock •

Kanawha •

Texas •

Powhatan •

Nottoway •

Meherrin •

Yadkin •

Catawba •

Mayo •

Toccoa • Enoree •

Tuskegee •

Apalachee •

Chickasaw • Miccosukee •

Pensacola •

Penobscot •

Norridgewock •

Nantucket •

Niantic • Raritan

Conestoga •

Delaware City •

Nanticoke •

Creeksville •

Sapona •

Pee Dee •

Stono •

Seminole •

Ocala •

Calusa Cove •

N

© 1994 DAVID JOURIS / PERIPHERAL VISION

49

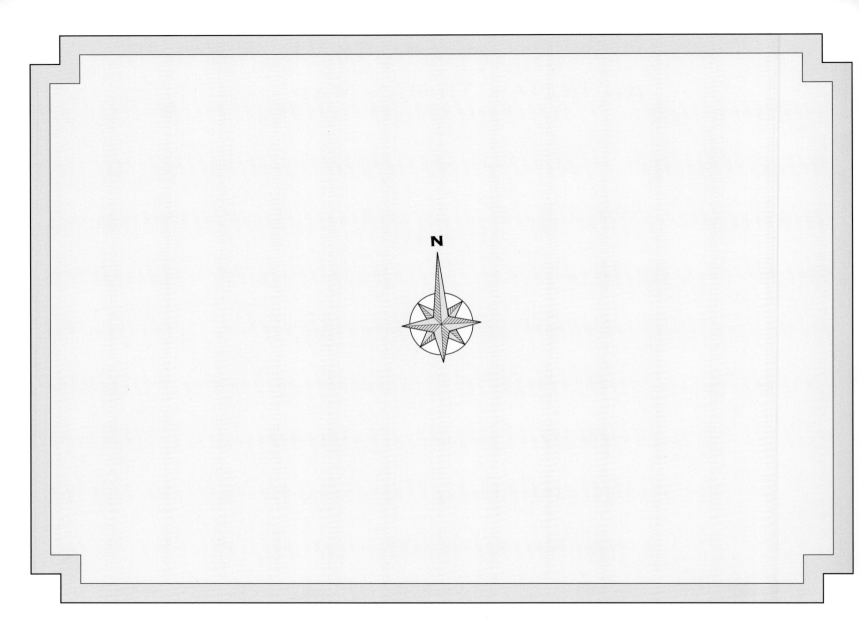

ECCENTRIC MAPS

Strangers in a Strange Land

> Eccentricity has always abounded when and where strength
> of character has abounded; and the amount of eccentricity
> in a society has been proportional to the amount of genius,
> mental vigor, and moral courage it contained.
> **—John Stuart Mill**

Normal, IL, took its name from Normal University, a teaching school set up there in the mid 1800s. In former times, teaching schools were often called "normal schools," a translation of the French term *école normale*. What "normal" means in this context is "standardized." In France, an *école normale* is a type of school that prepares future teachers by using a standardized curriculum. Before this type of government-supported school was set up in Paris in the late 1700s, anyone could open a school and teach their own views. It must be noted here that in the entire United States, a country of some 260,000,000 people, there are barely 40,000 Normal citizens. Now that's a statistic that speaks volumes.

In the neighboring state of Missouri, the official census lists some 1,500 Peculiar people. Obviously, **Peculiar, MO**, is not a town for the overly sensitive. The town got its name, so the story goes, when early residents of the community wrote to the Postmaster General to suggest several possibilities. When the residents were told that the proposed names were already in use by other towns in Missouri, they asked the Postmaster to choose a name for them, saying, "We don't care what name you give us, so long as it is sort of peculiar."

Around the turn of this century, residents in an area of Georgia that produced large quantities of green beans gathered to choose a name for their community. Unable to agree among themselves, the locals turned to a visiting bean merchant for an impartial decision. The merchant stated that naming a town was always an enigma, and thus, **Enigma, GA**, came to be. During a 1964 debate on much-needed voting reform, a young state senator from Enigma, appropriately enough, proposed with mock seriousness that no one be allowed to vote in Georgia elections "who has been deceased more than three years."

During the 1700s, French trappers navigated up the Ouachita River in southern Arkansas. Smackover Creek meets this river in an area dense with sumac. Apparently because the branches arched across the creek, the French referred to it as the *chemin couvert* (meaning "covered path"). To non–French-speaking newcomers, this name sounded like "Smackover." The original Smackover post office, near the mouth of the creek, was being permanently closed about the time the nearby town of Henderson, a few miles upstream, was asked to change its name due to a conflict of usage with a like-named Arkansas town. Since the townsfolk of Henderson were clearly up the creek without a name, it was suggested they take the name **Smackover, AR**. And they did.

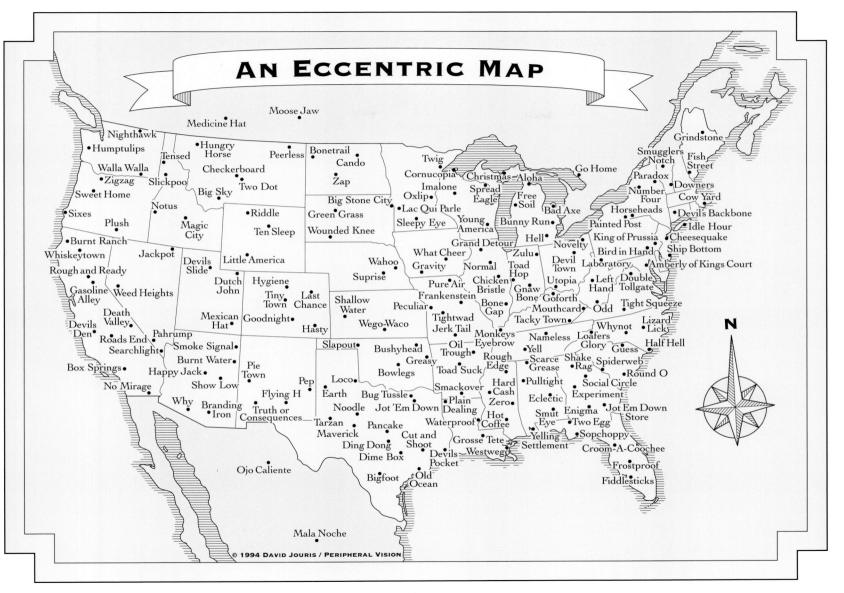

AN ECCENTRIC MAP

Moose Jaw

Medicine Hat

Nighthawk
Humptulips
Walla Walla
Zigzag
Sweet Home
Sixes
Plush
Burnt Ranch
Whiskeytown
Rough and Ready
Gasoline Alley
Weed Heights
Death Valley
Devils Den
Roads End
Searchlight
Box Springs
No Mirage
Happy Jack
Show Low
Why
Branding Iron
Truth or Consequences
Tarzan
Maverick
Ojo Caliente
Mala Noche

Tensed
Slickpoo
Notus
Jackpot
Pahrump
Smoke Signal
Burnt Water
Pie Town

Hungry Horse
Checkerboard
Big Sky
Magic City
Riddle
Ten Sleep
Devils Slide
Little America
Dutch John
Hygiene
Tiny Town
Mexican Hat
Goodnight
Flying H
Pep
Loco
Earth
Noodle
Pancake
Ding Dong
Dime Box
Bigfoot

Peerless
Two Dot

Bonetrail
Cando
Zap
Big Stone City
Green Grass
Wounded Knee
Wahoo
Suprise
Last Chance
Shallow Water
Hasty
Wego-Waco
Slapout
Bushyhead
Greasy
Bowlegs
Bug Tussle
Jot 'Em Down
Cut and Shoot
Old Ocean

Twig
Cornucopia
Imalone
Oxlip
Lac Qui Parle
Sleepy Eye
What Cheer
Gravity
Normal
Pure Air
Frankenstein
Peculiar
Tightwad
Jerk Tail
Oil Trough
Toad Suck
Smackover
Plain Dealing
Waterproof
Grosse Tete
Devils Pocket
Westwego

Christmas
Spread Eagle
Young America
Bunny Run
Grand Detour
Hell
Zulu
Chicken
Bristle
Bone Gap
Gnaw Bone
Monkeys Eyebrow
Rough Edge
Yell
Scarce Grease
Hard Cash
Zero
Hot Coffee
Yelling Settlement

Aloha
Free Soil
Bad Axe
Novelty
Devil Town
Utopia
Mouthcard
Tacky Town
Nameless
Loafers
Glory
Shake Rag
Pulltight
Eclectic
Smut Eye
Enigma
Two Egg
Sopchoppy
Croom-A-Coochee

Go Home

Number Four
Horseheads
Painted Post
King of Prussia
Bird in Hand
Laboratory
Left Hand
Goforth
Odd
Whynot
Guess
Spiderweb
Social Circle
Experiment
Jot Em Down Store
Frostproof
Fiddlesticks

Grindstone
Smugglers Notch
Paradox
Downers
Cow Yard
Devils Backbone
Idle Hour
Cheesequake
Ship Bottom
Amberly of Kings Court
Double Tollgate
Tight Squeeze
Lizard Lick
Half Hell
Round O

Fish Street

N

The truth is not ashamed of appearing contrived.
—ISAAC BASHEVIS SINGER

In true laconic style, there isn't much to say about the naming of **Sparta, IN**, or **Laconia, IN**. A few things are worth mentioning, however, about the original Laconia, an ancient Greek district, and Sparta, its capital. The citizens of Laconia were known for their brevity of speech. For example, when a triumphant Spartan general sent home the message, "Thebes is taken," his superiors informed him that "Taken" would have been sufficient. Another example occurred when Philip, King of Macedonia, was preparing to begin battle against the Spartans. Philip sent the message, "If I enter Laconia, I shall level Sparta." The Spartans' reply was a terse "If."

The interesting thing about **Democrat, NC**, is that it is located in Buncombe county. In 1820, a Democratic Congressman from Buncombe gave a speech in the House of Representatives during a debate on the Missouri Compromise. The Honorable Felix Walker delivered a long speech, noteworthy even in the hallowed halls of Congress for its irrelevance to the matter at hand. Walker later explained his actions by saying that he wasn't speaking for the benefit of the other Representatives, but for his constituency in Buncombe. Soon, the expression speaking for Buncombe came to refer to any long-winded, irrelevant speech. Over time the phrase was shortened to "bunkum," and finally to "bunk."

There used to be a town named Sink not so far away from the town of Drain, OR. Sink was named after a geographical feature, but Drain was the name of the family who founded the town. The area gets almost fifty inches of rain a year and the residents sometimes joke that the town is called Drain because that's where all the water comes down. Obviously the good folks in Drain haven't spent much time near Mt. Waialeale, HI, on the island of Kauai—a place that has ten times as much rain every year!

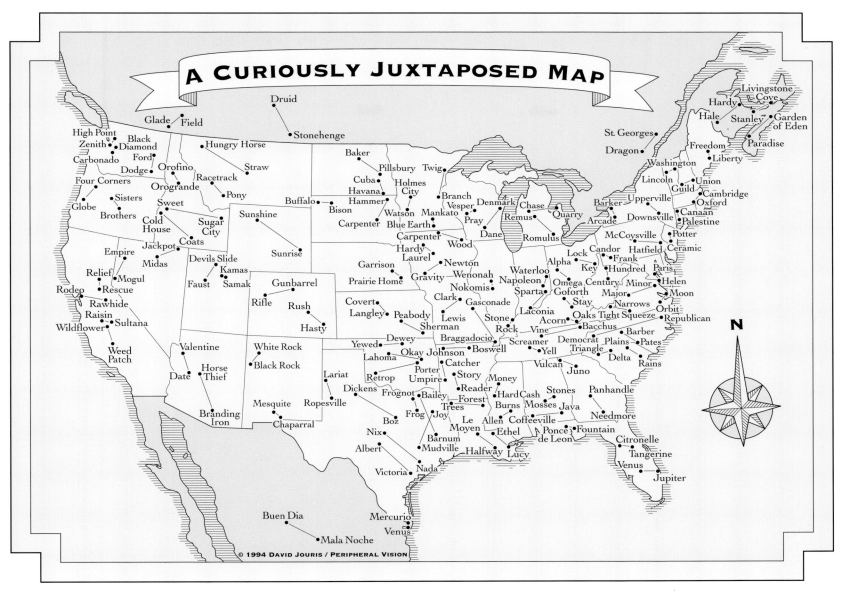

A Curiously Juxtaposed Map

My spelling is Wobbly. It's good spelling but it Wobbles,
and the letters get in the wrong places.
—A. A. MILNE

I don't see any use in spelling a word right and never did.
—MARK TWAIN

Residents of **Scircleville, IN**, will tell you that their town name isn't really misspelled. They claim it is named for one George Scircle. It is uncertain, however, whether George was much of a speller himself, so they seem to be taking a lot on faith.

In **El Granada, CA**, one senses, if not a war between the sexes, then at least a gender disagreement. Perhaps it's not so much bad spelling as bad grammar—the definite article in Spanish would correctly be "La," not "El."

The rather elegant sounding **Eltopia, WA**, is simply a creative spelling of "Hell-to-Pay." It resulted from a comment by a worker on a nearby railroad construction crew after learning that weeks of work spent grading the terrain had been washed away by heavy rains. Similarly, **Nuyaka, OK**, is thought to derive from the term "New Yorker," as translated by the Creek Indians.

Moores Hill, IN, began as Moore's Mill, but through an apparent transcription error, the second M turned into an H. Of course, the town is lucky that the "i" in their original name didn't also get changed—to an "e"—or their name would have really gone to hell. Cleveland, OH, was founded by a surveyor named Moses Cleaveland in 1796. Some thirty-five years later, a newspaper printer misspelled the name, leaving out the first "a," and the city has been spelled Cleveland ever since. Still, it may be just coincidence that residents of Cleveland sometimes refer to their city as "the mistake by the lake."

Speaking of which, there is a lake in south central Massachusetts that is sometimes called Lake Webster because its proper name is difficult to spell and a bit of a mouthful to say. In point of fact, almost every printed reference to the lake seems to use a different spelling. The correct spelling is: Lake Chargoggagoggmanchauggagoggchaubunagungamaugg. The popular translation of the Algonquian name is, "You fish on your side; I fish on my side; nobody fishes in the middle." The lake is near the town of Webster, MA. This town is the namesake of Daniel Webster who probably wouldn't be pleased at the notion that there isn't enough room to put the lake's name on the map. It was Webster, after all, who, when advised that it might not be smart for him to try to join the already overcrowded profession of law, quipped, "There is always room at the top."

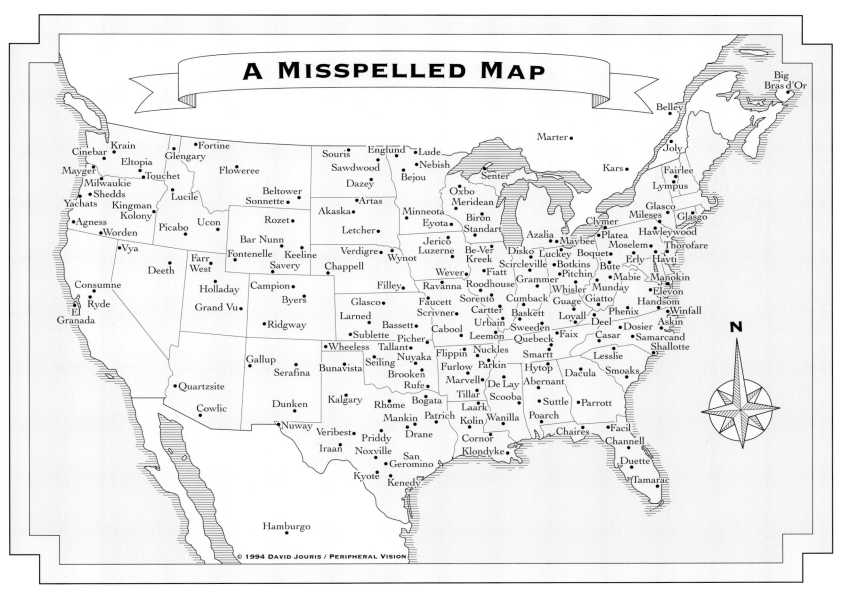

A MISSPELLED MAP

Big Bras d'Or

Belley

Marter

Joly

Kars

Fairlee
Lympus

Cinebar   Krain   Fortine
Glengary
Eltopia
Mayger   Touchet
Milwaukie   Floweree
Shedds
Yachats   Beltower
Kingman   Sonnette
Kolony   Lucile
Agness   Picabo   Ucon
Worden
Vya

Souris   Englund   Lude
Sawdwood   Nebish
Dazey   Bejou
Artas
Akaska
Letcher
Minneota
Eyota

Senter

Oxbo
Meridean
Biron
Standart

Glasco
Mileses   Glasgo
Clymer   Platea   Hawleywood
Azalia   Moselem   Thorofare
Disko Luckey Boquet
Scircleville Botkins   Erly   Hayti
Grammer   Pitchin   Bute
Whisler   Munday   Mabie   Manokin
Elevon
Handsom
Phenix   Winfall
Deel   Dosier   Askin

Rozet
Deeth   Farr
West
Holladay   Campion
Grand Vu   Byers

Bar Nunn
Fontenelle   Keeline
Savery
Chappell
Verdigre
Wynot

Jerico
Luzerne
Be-Ver
Kreek
Wever   Fiatt
Ravanna   Roodhouse
Sorento
Faucett   Cumback   Guage   Giatto
Scrivner   Cartter   Baskett   Loyall
Urbain   Sweeden
Leemon   Quebeck   Faix
Casar   Samarcand
Shallotte

Consume
Ryde
El
Granada

Filley
Glasco
Larned
Bassett
Picher
Sublette   Tallant
Wheeless
Cabool

Smartt
Lesslie
Smoaks

Gallup
Serafina
Bunavista
Seiling   Nuyaka
Brooken
Rufe

Flippin   Nuckles
Furlow   Parkin
Marvell   De Lay   Abernant
Scooba
Hytop
Dacula   Parrott
Suttle

Ridgway

Quartzsite

Cowlic

Dunken
Kalgary
Rhome
Mankin
Drane

Bogata
Patrick
Laark
Kolin

Tillar
Wanilla
Poarch
Chaires
Facil
Channell

Nuway
Veribest   Priddy
Iraan   Noxville
San
Geromino
Kyote   Kenedy

Cornor
Klondyke

Duette
Tamarac

Hamburgo

© 1994 David Jouris / Peripheral Vision

N

And after it rains there's a rainbow, and all of the colors are black.
It's not that the colors aren't there, it's just imagination they lack.
Everything's the same back in my little town.
—**PAUL SIMON**, "My Little Town"

Imagination is more important than knowledge.
—**ALBERT EINSTEIN**

When local investors gathered together to choose a name for a new community in eastern Alabama, everyone seemed to have his or her own favorite, and no one could come to an agreement. Finally one man made a moving plea for accord, asking the others to alter their perspective and think, "not my town, not your town, but our town." And on that, they all agreed; that was the beginning of **Our Town, AL**.

Village, VA, was formerly named Union Village because it was on the border of two counties. Records show the community was still being called Union Village in 1857, but by 1884, it was just Village. One theory is that the name was changed because in the South, after the Civil War, anything with the word "union" in it was asking for trouble. It is perhaps unfair to suggest that this community has always appeared unimaginative, since prior to taking the name Union Village the town was called Burnt Chimneys.

Some authorities, such as the editors of *Webster's Dictionary*, think that the commonly used meaning of the word "podunk"— a small, out-of-the-way place of no account—may have actually come from the little community of **Podunk, MA**. The word in question probably derives from an Algonquian Indian word used to describe a geographical location on "a neck of land."

Halfway, OR, was so named because it was halfway between two well-known towns—Pine and Cornucopia. As sometimes happens, however, the town has moved since its founding and is no longer halfway between the two points.

The small community of **Center City, TX**, is the home of Center Oak, a tree that still stands and marks, according to legend, the exact center of the great state of Texas. Precisely how one would determine the exact center of Texas, let alone why, is something best not gone into here.

Plain City, OH, was formerly named Pleasant Valley. Apparently the citizens *never* let their imagination get the best of them.

An Unimaginative Map

© 1994 David Jouris / Peripheral Vision

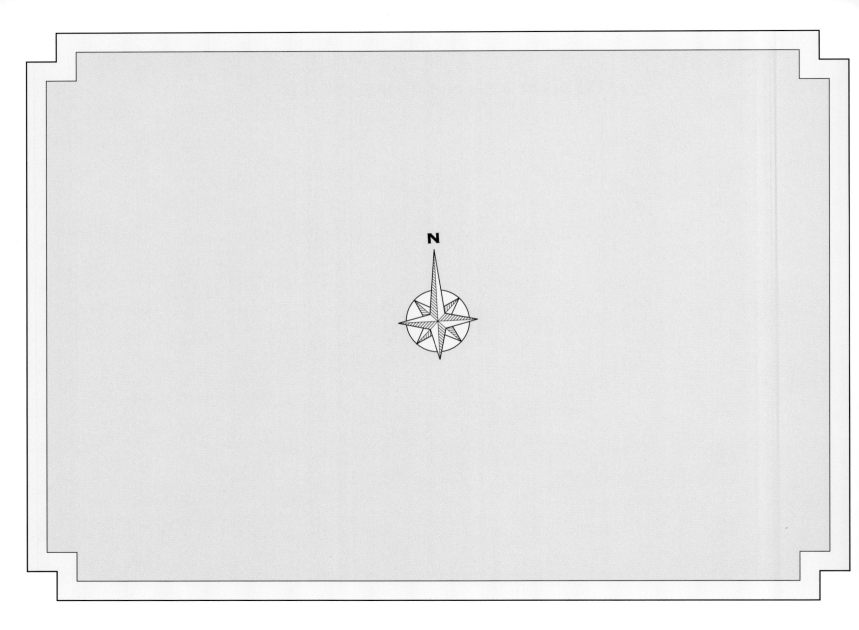

EVERYDAY MAPS

Edible Journeys and a Number of Others

Food is an important part of a balanced diet.
—FRAN LEBOWITZ

Looks can be deceiving—it's eating that's believing.
—JAMES THURBER

The community of **Rabbit Hash, KY**, is said to have taken its name from the severe lack of choice on the menu of the early settlers. Apparently, rabbits were hunted easily in this area along the Ohio River, especially during times when the river would flood and send the rabbits scampering to higher ground. There is a folk story told about a traveler waiting on the Indiana side of the river who inquired if there was anything to eat at the landing on the other side. "Plenty of rabbit hash," he was told. When a post office was established at the landing, the residents felt this was an apt name for their little village.

Pie Town, NM, got its name because a baker, known for his pies, advertised his specialty with a big sign on the highway at this site. Although this small town probably isn't large enough to have an elite class, one has a keen suspicion of what they would be called if it did. Alas, now there's no filling or lower crust either, as pies are no longer being sold in Pie Town.

In order to be able to receive mail directly in their own community, the residents of what is now **Tomato, AR**, gathered in the general store to decide on a name. It's said that during the discussion, a young woman happened to look at a can of tomatoes and suggested "Tomato" as the name. Local historians have no trouble accepting this story; as far as they are concerned, all of the controversy centers upon who the young woman was.

There are two principle theories on how **Chewsville, MD**, got its name. The first is that the town was named by Colonel Peregrine Fitzhugh for the Chew family. Fitzhugh was about as close to the family as he could get without being born into it—his wife was a Chew daughter. There are also strong proponents of the theory that "Chew" was a mistaken pronunciation of the name Fitzhugh. If so, one can imagine that the garbled version occurred when someone heard the name Fitzhugh from a person who was talking with their mouth full.

Gnaw Bone, IN, despite some of the colorful stories one could imagine, seems most likely to be named after the French city of Narbonne.

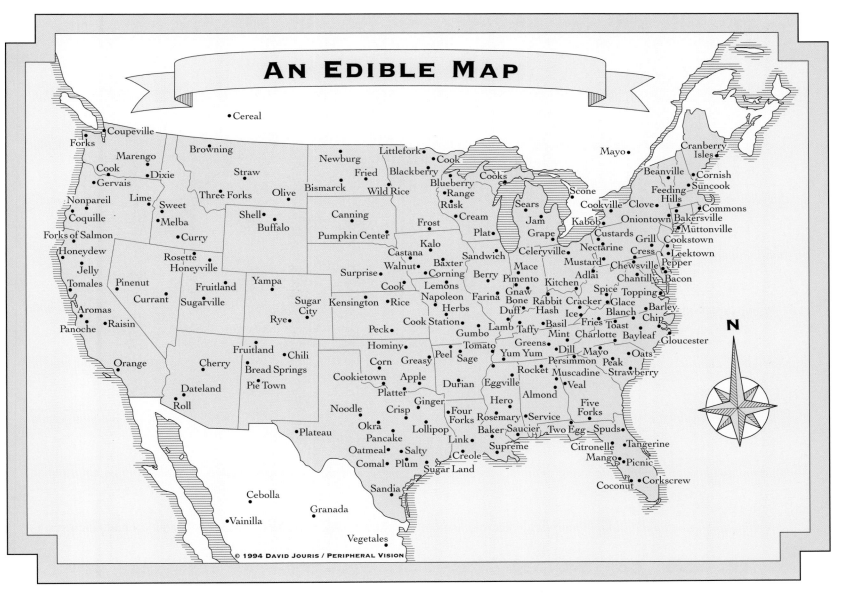

AN EDIBLE MAP

© 1994 David Jouris / Peripheral Vision

Work has been a game all my life. It's been more fun than
I could possibly tell you. It has been like being in love.
—**BEATRICE WARDE**

Incomprehensible jargon is the hallmark of a profession.
—**KINGMAN BREWSTER**

The town of **Matador, TX**, was named after the Matador Ranch, the largest land holding in the region. Matador became a town without actually being one—rather, it was a *Potemkin village*. When the handful of residents in the area wanted to create a county and establish Matador as the county seat, they were informed by government officials that, to qualify, the town had to have at least twenty businesses. Since the townsite only had one business—a saloon—some ranch hands briefly set up phony business fronts, using supplies borrowed from the ranch, and managed to succeed in having their "town" named as the county seat.

The site of a trading post since the mid 1800s, **Chapman, KS**, takes its name from a local creek named by Horace Greeley. The appellation was chosen by Greeley as a reference to the nearby store. Meaning merchant or trader, "chapman" derives from the Anglo-Saxon *céap* (meaning "barter, trade").

Secretary, MD, takes its name from Secretary Sewell Creek. This creek had been named in honor of Lord Henry Sewell, an English settler who was Secretary of the Province of Maryland in the latter part of the seventeenth century. (A note for travelers: even though it is a small town of fewer than 500 people, there is at least one business establishment in Secretary that *does* make coffee.)

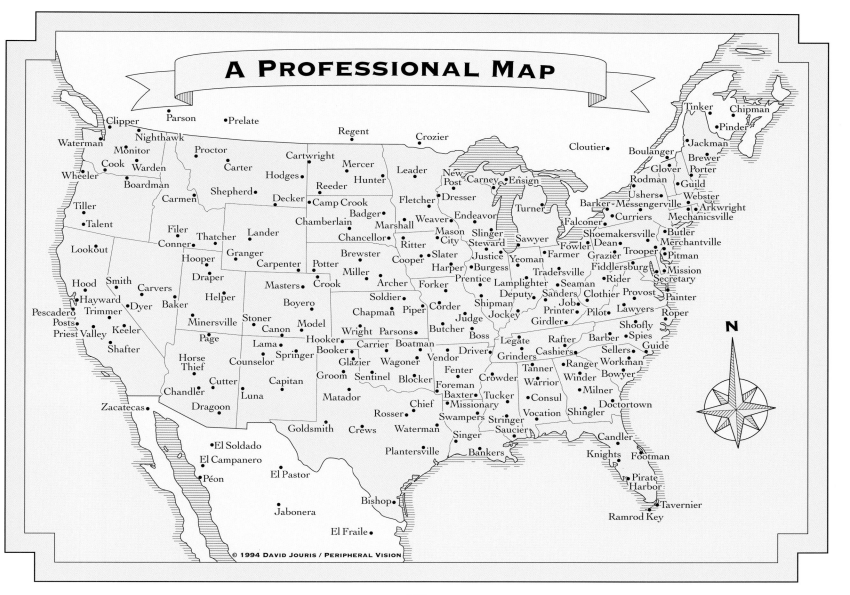

A PROFESSIONAL MAP

I look upon them as dangerous and tiring activities performed by
people with whom I share nothing except the right to trial by jury.
—**Fran Lebowitz**, *on sports*

The English are not a very spiritual people. So they invented
cricket to give them some idea of eternity.
—**George Bernard Shaw**

Rugby, ND, is named for Rugby, England. Giving its name to a North Dakota town is not what the English town is best known for, however; previously it had bestowed its name on its own Rugby School. This school is where the sport of rugby was first played, developed by a student who habitually ignored the established rules of soccer. By the way, for those suffering from thalassophobia, Rugby, ND, is the location of the geographical center of North America.

The town founder chose the name **Tenstrike, MN**, near the turn of this century; it is commonly thought that he was making reference to a term in the sport of bowling, namely to knock down all ten pins with one ball. The word "tenstrike," however, was also used in common parlance at the time to mean "a highly successful achievement." Given the dearth of bowling pins in Minnesota in those days, the smart money is riding on the theory that the founder was simply patting himself on the back.

There are three stories that tell how **Bowling Green, KY**, was named. The most common tale is that the town got its name from a "ball alley" where locals bowled for recreation. A problem with this explanation is that the terrain wasn't flat (a big drawback for bowlers), and, since the land wasn't settled yet, there was no one there to enjoy the sport. The second story alleges that the town was named after Bowling Green, VA. Unfortunately, although there were many settlers from Virginia that moved westward into Kentucky, they came mostly from the western part of Virginia, not from the eastern side where Bowling Green, VA, is located. Our third, and favored, explanation is that the town was honoring Bowling Green Square in New York City. The people who named the town were the same folks who named Warren County, of which Bowling Green is the county seat. The county had been named for General Joseph Warren, an American patriot who was killed in 1775 at the Battle of Bunker Hill. The significance of Bowling Green Square is that a statue of George III that stood there was melted down and made into bullets for use by the Americans during the Revolutionary War.

Golf, FL, was founded by the same chaps who developed **Golf, IL**. It doesn't take a rocket scientist to realize what the founders had on their mind, although perhaps they simply felt that consistency was a virtue.

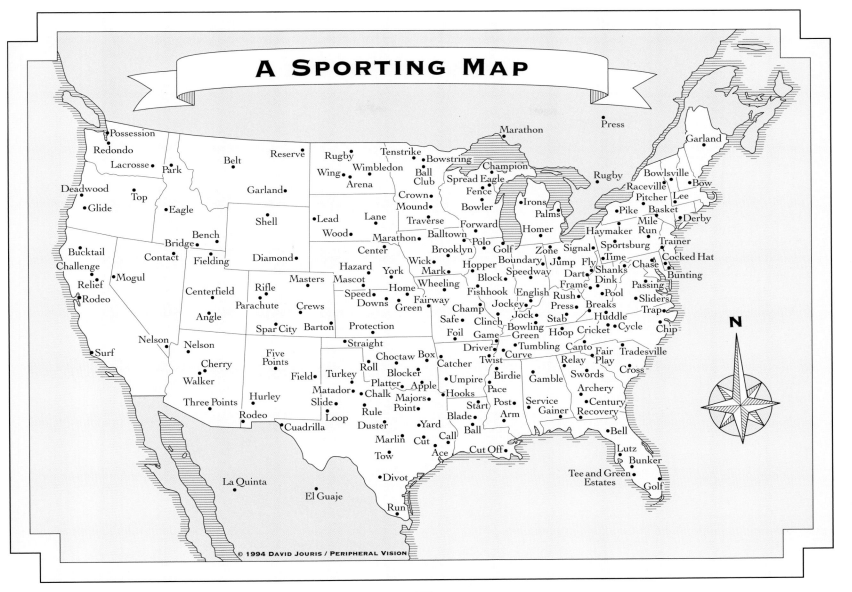

A SPORTING MAP

© 1994 DAVID JOURIS / PERIPHERAL VISION

> Numbers constitute the only universal language.
> **—NATHANAEL WEST**

> Never insult seven men when all you're packin' is a six-gun.
> **—ATTRIBUTED TO ZANE GREY**

Double Adobe, AZ, was named for a local two-room adobe building, built with eighteen-inch thick walls and several openings through which to shoot guns. Double Adobe was the kind of place that put the word "wild" in the term "wild west."

Two Dot, MT, is named for the brand used by a local cattle rancher. The brand consisted of a big dot on the shoulder and a second dot on the thigh, which were difficult for cattle rustlers to alter.

During the depression it wasn't uncommon for children in rural areas to be given eggs to trade for treats at their local store. In the community of **Two Egg, FL**, it's said that little children would come into the shop, extend their barter saying "two egg" to describe the usual quantity they wished to trade, and await the exchange for candy.

You'll find **Eighty Eight, KY**, 8.8 miles southeast of Glasgow, the county seat of Barren County, and that's how the name originated. The postmaster claimed his penmanship was poor, so instead of writing out the word "Eighty Eight," he just used the number *88*. The Postal Service frowns on this kind of thing nowadays.

The longevity of two residents—Henry Church, who lived to be 109, and his wife, who reached 106—is said to have been the inspiration for the name of **Hundred, WV**.

The expression "one-horse town" comes from the time when horses were the principal means of hauling and transportation. A place that needed only one horse to do the necessary hauling was really small. This should give you some indication of the population in the rural community of **One Horse Store, AR**.

Residents of **Two Taverns, PA**, didn't overlook the obvious, either. They named the community for the presence of two taverns, located there since the eighteenth century. Two other communities with fairly straightforward name origins are **Eighty Four, PA**—named because the local post office was established there in 1884—and **Fifty-Six, AR**—which is located in the 56th state school district.

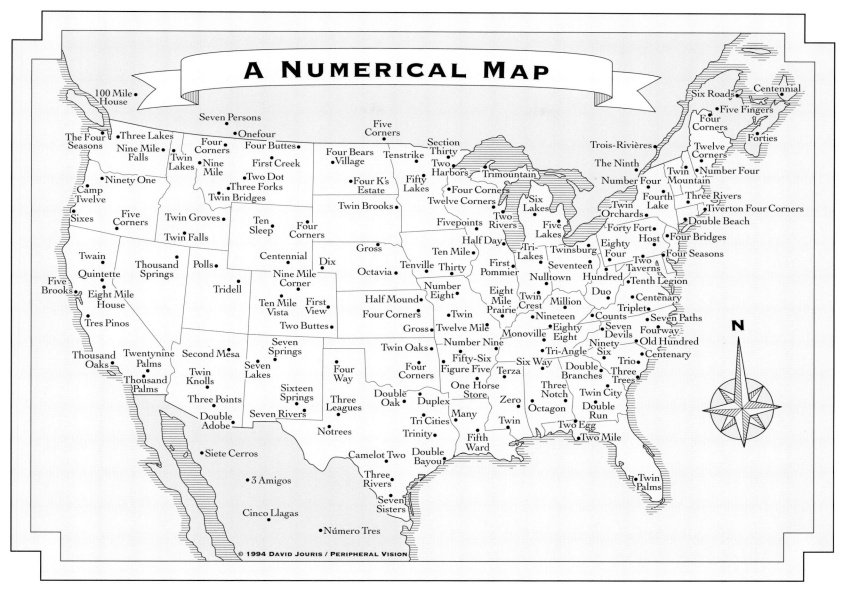

A NUMERICAL MAP

© 1994 David Jouris / Peripheral Vision

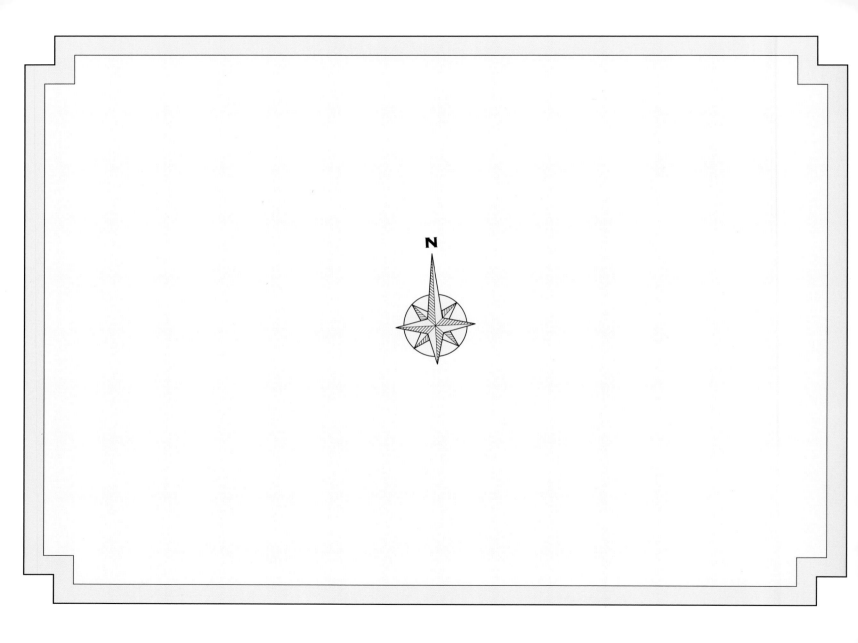

PERSONAL MAPS

Public Figures and Private Investigations

Egotist: a person of low taste, more interested in himself than in me.
—**Ambrose Bierce**

There is no human problem which could not be solved if people would simply do as I advise.
—**Gore Vidal**

I am the greatest.
—**Muhammad Ali**

The rural community of **Dolly Varden, OH**, is said to be named after a character created by Charles Dickens, in his novel *Barnaby Rudge*. Dolly Varden was known for wearing bright colors and a decorated hat. Her style of dress spawned a fashion trend in the nineteenth century that lasted for decades. In the 1870s, when the Dickens novel was popular, the name was also bestowed on a colorful trout that has olive-green scales with red-orange dots.

Formerly named Mauch Chunk (of Algonquian Indian origin, meaning "bear mountain"), the town of **Jim Thorpe, PA**, was renamed in honor of the great Native American athlete. Thorpe, who competed in the 1912 Olympic Games in Stockholm, Sweden, and took first place in both the decathlon and pentathlon, had attended Carlisle Industrial School, an Indian boarding school in Pennsylvania.

Helen Furnace, PA, is not actually named for a woman. It seems there was a company—Hieland Furnace—that was so named because an early settler named McNaughton boasted of being a Hielander (i.e., a person from the Highlands of Scotland). Over time, the name was corrupted to Helen Furnace.

There are three small communities named **Jenny Lind**—in **CA**, **AR**, and **NC**—in honor of the famous Swedish singer who toured the United States in the mid 1800s, under the management of P. T. Barnum. Obviously "the Swedish Nightingale," as she was popularly known, made quite an impact on the populace from coast to coast.

A local ballad entitled "Ben Bolt and Sweet Alice," provided inspiration for the town of **Ben Bolt, TX**. The name is particularly appropriate since there is a town named Alice, TX, only a few miles away.

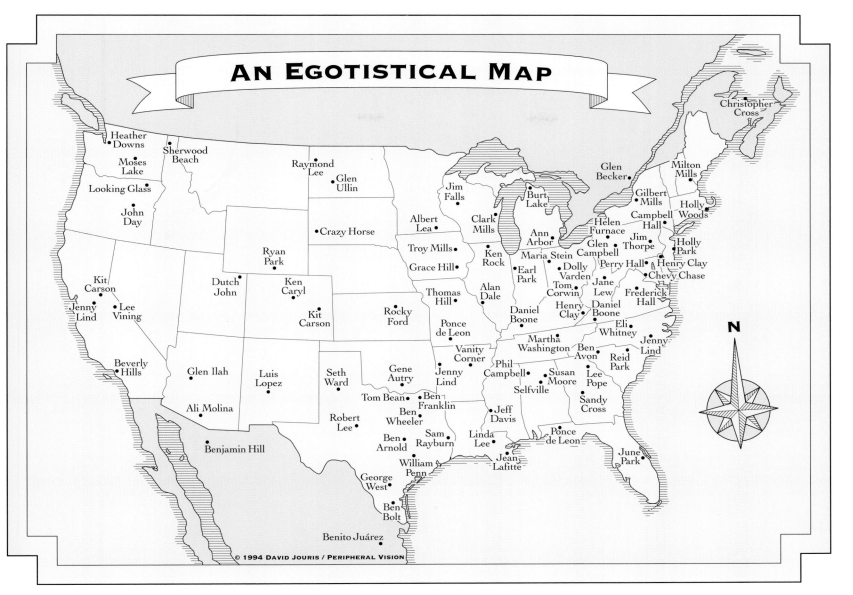

AN EGOTISTICAL MAP

Christopher Cross

Heather Downs

Sherwood Beach

Moses Lake

Looking Glass

John Day

Raymond Lee

Glen Ullin

Glen Becker

Milton Mills

Jim Falls

Burt Lake

Gilbert Mills

Holly Woods

Albert Lea

Clark Mills

Campbell Hall

Crazy Horse

Ann Arbor

Helen Furnace

Glen Campbell

Jim Thorpe

Holly Park

Ryan Park

Troy Mills

Ken Rock

Maria Stein

Perry Hall

Henry Clay

Grace Hill

Earl Park

Dolly Varden

Chevy Chase

Kit Carson

Dutch John

Ken Caryl

Thomas Hill

Alan Dale

Tom Corwin

Jane Lew

Frederick Hall

Jenny Lind

Lee Vining

Kit Carson

Rocky Ford

Ponce de Leon

Daniel Boone

Henry Clay

Daniel Boone

Eli Whitney

Jenny Lind

Martha Washington

Ben Avon

Reid Park

Beverly Hills

Glen Ilah

Luis Lopez

Seth Ward

Gene Autry

Vanity Corner

Jenny Lind

Phil Campbell

Susan Moore

Lee Pope

Ali Molina

Selfville

Sandy Cross

Tom Bean

Ben Franklin

Benjamin Hill

Ben Wheeler

Jeff Davis

Robert Lee

Sam Rayburn

Linda Lee

Ponce de Leon

Ben Arnold

June Park

William Penn

Jean Lafitte

George West

Ben Bolt

Benito Juárez

N

Anatomy is to physiology as geography to history;
it describes the theatre of events.
—**JEAN F. FERNEL**

I've got you under my skin,
I've got you deep in the heart of me.
—**COLE PORTER**, "I've Got You Under My Skin"

There are numerous springs in the region around **Sweet Lips, TN**, and the story goes that one of the early settlers arriving in this place stopped to drink from one of them. When a companion asked him how the water tasted, he replied that it was "sweet to the lips."

The town of **Scarville, IA**, was named for Ole Scar, a fellow of Norwegian descent who owned most of the land there and whose mercantile store was one of the first businesses in town. He also helped found the bank and donated land for the town's first schoolhouse. Scar was obviously a cut above the usual settler.

Heart Mountain, WY, is a translation of the Crow Indian name for the nearby mountain (*Awaxaamnaasé*, meaning "heart"), because of its shape. Ironically, reflecting a decided lack of heart on the part of the United States government and the majority of its citizens, this rural community was the location, during WWII, of a concentration camp where more than 10,000 Americans of Japanese descent were interned.

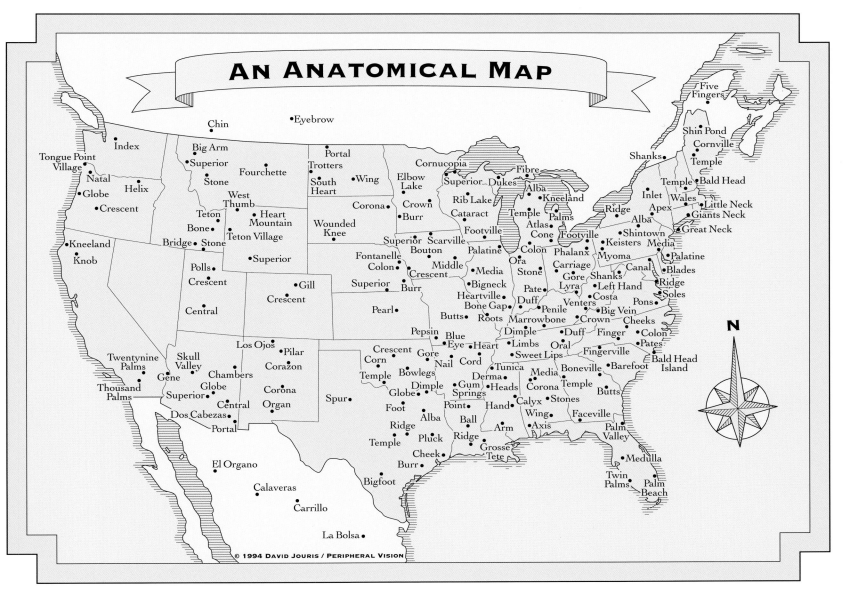

An Anatomical Map

© 1994 David Jouris / Peripheral Vision

Lolita, TX, was named in 1910 for a local resident, Lolita Reese. The name was almost changed in the 1950s, when the notoriety of Vladimir Nabokov's satirical novel, *Lolita*—concerning the relationship between a twelve-year-old nymphet and a middle-aged professor—scandalized the town.

The town of **Annville, PA**, named for the wife of the town founder, has been known to employ an anvil as its logo—not because the local industry was metal forging, but as a pronunciation guide for those who might have a tendency to draw out the last syllable of the town's name as if it rhymed with "will."

Florence, MT, not a large community, used to be a real one-horse town. And it was so named—One Horse.

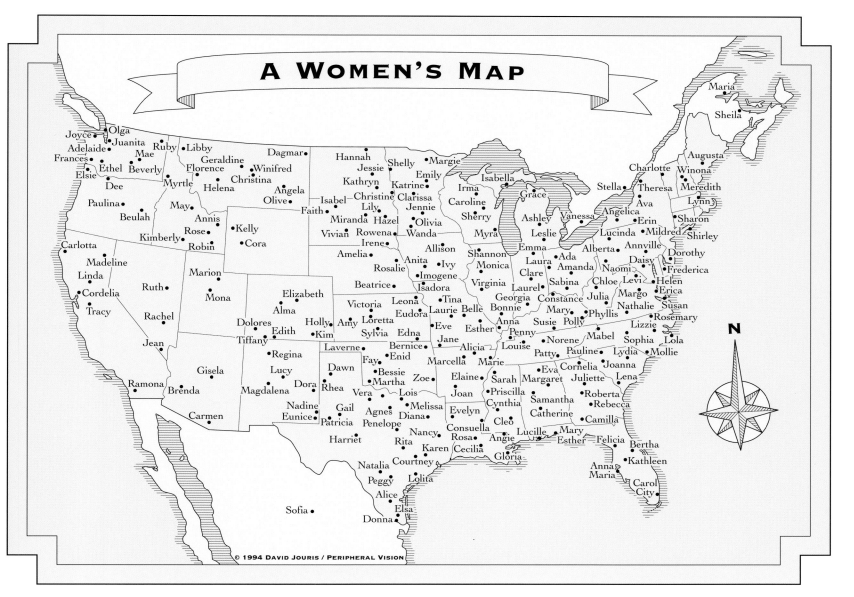

A WOMEN'S MAP

© 1994 DAVID JOURIS / PERIPHERAL VISION

A man got to do what he got to do.
—**JOHN STEINBECK**

Q: Do you consider yourself militant?
A: I consider myself Malcolm.
—INTERVIEW WITH **MALCOLM X**

The name **Marvin, SD**, is actually taken from the brand name of the office safe at the train depot, where the locals had gathered to come up with a name for their town. The residents were searching for something that was relatively short, not already in use elsewhere in the state, and acceptable to everyone. The man who proposed calling the town Marvin theorized that this would be a "safe" name to use.

Joes, CO, was originally named for three settlers named Joe. For some years, before the town streamlined its name, it was called Three Joes.

It would be a shame to leave this theme without mentioning the town of Avon, CO. When a new bridge was built over the Eagle River here, the town council was given a number of suggestions for names for the span. In its wisdom, after considering the suggestions put forward, the council made its choice: "Bob." With no dissent from the citizenry, the name was made official. Demonstrating an uncommon sense of follow-through, the town then celebrated by holding a *Bob-B-Que.*

Finally, in another slight digression, there are some rather interesting changes that have taken place in the family names of some well-known men. Paul Revere, for example, came from a French family named Rivoire. His father changed the spelling to Revere so that, well, in his own words, "the bumpkins can pronounce it easier." Irving Berlin's last name was originally Baline. General Custer came from a family named Köster, World War I's General Pershing was from a family named Pfoersching, and Huber was the original name of President Herbert Hoover's family.

A MEN'S MAP

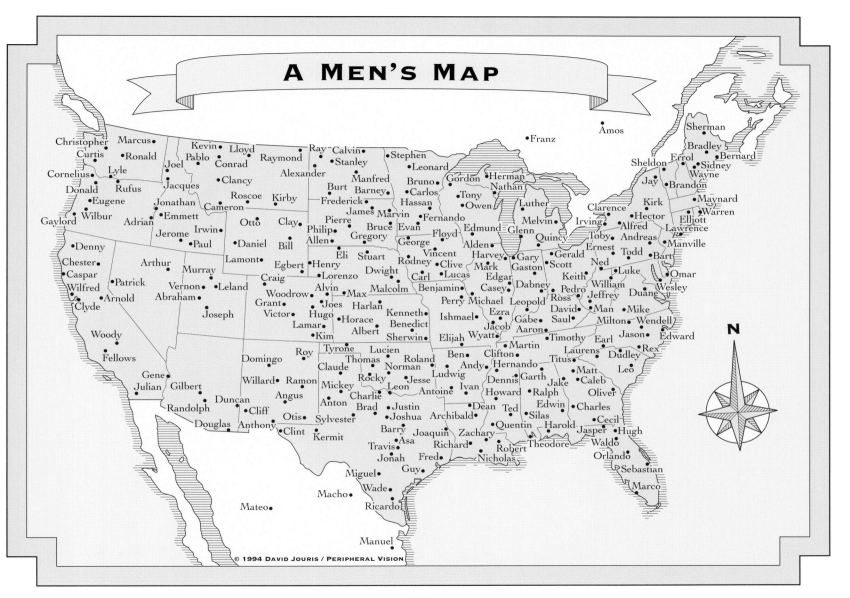

© 1994 DAVID JOURIS / PERIPHERAL VISION

I've got road maps from two dozen states.
I've got coast to coast just to contemplate.
Will you still love me when I get back to town?
—**JONI MITCHELL**, "Blue Motel Room"

If we're gonna change the world, the first
thing we gotta do is change our hearts.
—**JAMES BROWN**

Sparks, GA, was named for a Mr. Sparks who was an official of the railroad that served the region. The interesting thing about Sparks is its relationship to the nearby town of Adel. Adel, GA, is said to have gotten its name when the first postmaster removed the first and last four letters from Philadelphia, apparently feeling that there wasn't enough dignity in the town's original name—Puddleville. The poor man was fighting an uphill battle, however, as residents took to saying with some fondness that "Adel is so close to *Hell* you can see Sparks."

Earlier in the century there was a place named Chocolate in North Carolina. Was it only coincidence that the post office there first opened on February 14, 1921, and closed just over nine months later? In this same area a post office named Passion also once existed. It is well documented that Passion lasted for little more than five years. Make of all this what you will, but keep in mind that even science has now managed to come up with a link between chocolate and feelings of love. (In the same county there is a small mountain called Chocolate Drop. Seems to be quite a sweet tooth in that region.)

In the mid 1970s, the town of Deerfield, IL, created *Kissing* and *No Kissing* passenger drop-off zones at their train station. The signs are still in use, and souvenir copies of each sign are now available. Although romantics might imagine that the *Kissing* sign would easily outsell its competition, sales are reported to be neck and neck, so to speak.

Climax, CO, is situated at the summit of the pass over Mt. Lincoln—the "high point" of the train ride for passengers headed to the gold and silver mines in the area.

A LOVERS' MAP

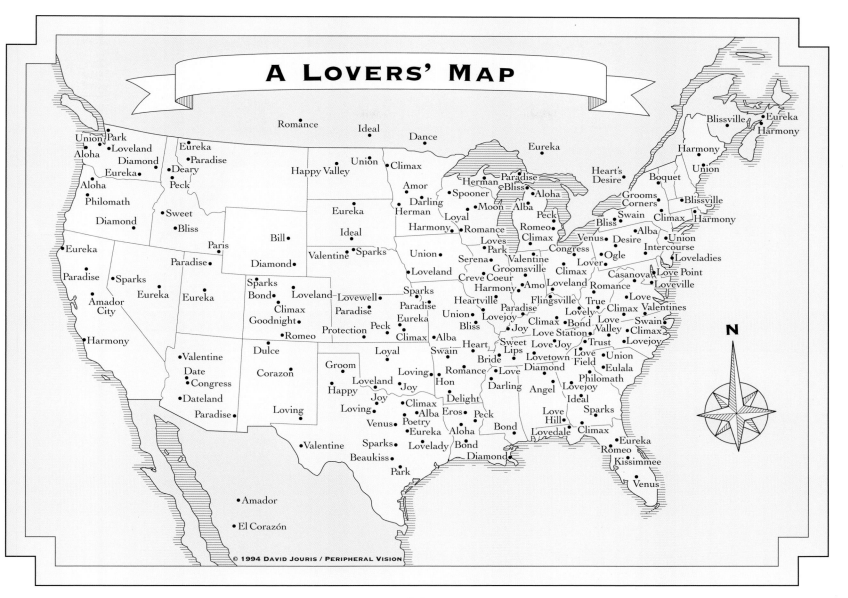

Romance Ideal Dance Eureka Blissville • Eureka

Union Park Eureka Harmony Harmony

Aloha Loveland Paradise Union

Diamond Deary Happy Valley Union Climax Heart's Desire Boquet

Eureka Peck Amor Spooner Paradise Bliss Grooms Corners

Aloha Darling Moon Alba Swain Blissville

Philomath Sweet Herman Loyal Peck Romeo Bliss Climax Harmony

Diamond Bliss Eureka Harmony Romance Climax Venus Desire Alba Union

Bill Ideal Loves Congress Lover Ogle Loveladies

Paris Valentine Sparks Union Park Valentine Climax Casanova Love Point

Eureka Diamond Loveland Serena Groomsville Loveland Romance Loveville

Paradise Sparks Creve Coeur Amo True Love

Sparks Loveland Lovewell Harmony Flingsville Climax Valentines

Amador City Bond Climax Paradise Heartville Paradise Lovely Love Swain

Eureka Eureka Goodnight Protection Peck Eureka Union Lovejoy Climax Bond Valley Climax

Harmony Romeo Climax Bliss Joy Love Station Trust Lovejoy

Dulce Loyal Alba Heart Sweet Lips Love Joy

Valentine Groom Loving Swain Bride Lovetown Love Field Union

Date Corazon Loveland Romance Love Diamond Eulala

Congress Happy Joy Hon Darling Angel Lovejoy Philomath

Dateland Joy Delight Ideal

Paradise Loving Climax Eros Peck Love Hill Sparks

Venus Poetry Aloha Bond Lovedale Climax

Valentine Sparks Eureka Bond Eureka

Amador Beaukiss Lovelady Diamond Romeo Kissimmee

El Corazón Park Venus

N

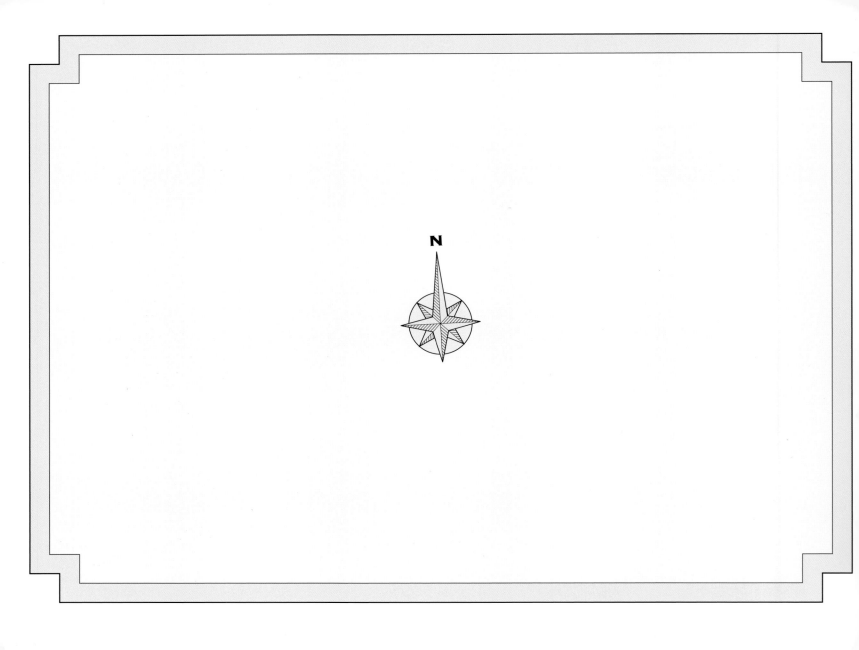

MISCELLANEOUS MAPS

*Themes That Came to Mind While En Route
to That Place in the South of France*

Things are going to get a lot worse before they get worse.
—**LILY TOMLIN**

My pessimism goes to the point of suspecting the sincerity
of the pessimists.
—**JEAN ROSTAND**

Yes, there are cold days in Hell. And there are times when Hell does freeze over. **Hell, MI**, got its name from its founder, George Reeves, in an unguarded moment. Reeves had been chatting with a group of friends, when someone asked him what they ought to call the community he'd built up around his flour mill. "I don't care, call it Hell if you want to," he replied. In later years, the presence of a distillery and tavern in Hell—and the resulting drunkenness and brawls—seemed like an attempt by the town to live up (down?) to its name.

The town of **Accident, MD**, may create more than its share of unintentional confusion. A state highway runs right through the center of town, so drivers unfamiliar with the area are likely to be very cautious after seeing the town sign proclaiming "Accident." If there is a car problem, it can be dealt with at the appropriately named Accident Garage. Pessimists would not be surprised to find that the local physician is located on Cemetery Road. And one wonders if the good doctor is missing a bet by not proclaiming that he is the "Accident M.D. of Accident, MD." The town got its name when the land was opened for settlement by Lord Baltimore in 1774. Two different parties coincidentally surveyed the same section of land, near to where the town is now located. One of the principals acknowledged that they had both chosen the same tract "by accident," but he magnanimously agreed to relinquish any right to the property since the other claimant was a friend of his. The county records show the land was henceforth named "The Accident Tract."

Gripe, AZ, was named by employees at the agricultural inspection station that is located there in order to safeguard against unwanted animal and vegetable pests that might otherwise enter the state with motorists driving across the New Mexico border. It is uncertain whether the name came about because motorists were likely to gripe when they were stopped by inspectors, or because the inspectors spent a lot of time griping about their job. Pessimists would assume, of course, that both parties were griping.

Col. August Hazard gave his name to the community of **Hazardville, CT**. He was also the founder of the Hazard Powder Company that began there in 1835. This company proved to be aptly named when, after a few smaller explosions, it finally went out of business with a *big* bang in the early 1900s—taking several employees with it.

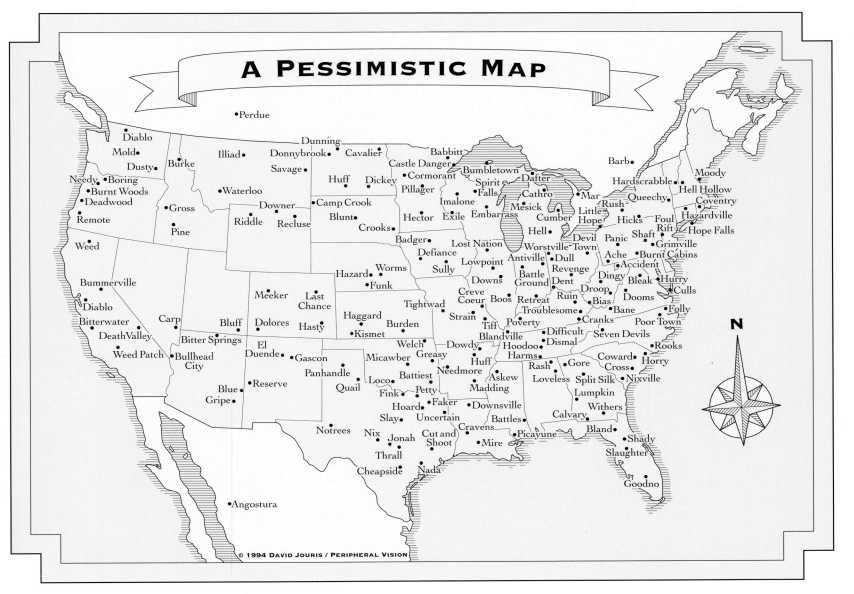

A Pessimistic Map

Perdue • Diablo • Mold • Dusty • Burke • Illiad • Dunning • Donnybrook • Cavalier • Savage • Castle Danger • Cormorant • Bumbletown • Spirit Falls • Dafter • Babbitt • Barb • Moody • Hardscrabble • Needy • Boring • Burnt Woods • Deadwood • Waterloo • Huff • Dickey • Pillager • Imalone • Mesick • Cathro • Mar • Rush • Queechy • Hell Hollow • Coventry • Gross • Downer • Camp Crook • Blunt • Hector • Exile • Embarrass • Cumber • Little Hope • Hicks • Foul Rift • Hazardville • Hope Falls • Remote • Pine • Riddle • Recluse • Crooks • Badger • Hell • Devil Town • Panic • Shaft • Grimville • Weed • Lost Nation • Worstville • Ache • Burnt Cabins • Defiance • Lowpoint • Antiville • Dull • Revenge • Accident • Hazard • Worms • Sully • Downs • Battle Ground • Dent • Dingy • Bleak • Hurry • Culls • Bummerville • Funk • Creve Coeur • Boos • Retreat • Ruin • Droop • Bias • Dooms • Folly • Diablo • Meeker • Last Chance • Tightwad • Strain • Troublesome • Cranks • Bane • Poor Town • Bitterwater • Haggard • Burden • Tiff • Poverty • Difficult • Seven Devils • Death Valley • Carp • Bluff • Dolores • Hasty • Kismet • Welch • Dowdy • Blandville • Hoodoo • Dismal • Rooks • Bitter Springs • El Duende • Gascon • Micawber • Greasy • Harms • Coward • Horry • Weed Patch • Bullhead City • Panhandle • Loco • Battiest • Needmore • Huff • Rash • Gore • Cross • Nixville • Blue Gripe • Reserve • Quail • Fink • Petty • Askew • Madding • Loveless • Split Silk • Lumpkin • Hoard • Faker • Downsville • Battles • Calvary • Withers • Notrees • Nix • Slay • Uncertain • Cravens • Picayune • Bland • Shady • Jonah • Cut and Shoot • Mire • Slaughter • Thrall • Cheapside • Nada • Goodno • Angostura

N

Where seldom is heard a discouraging word,
And the skies are not cloudy all day.
—ATTRIBUTED TO **BREWSTER HIGLEY**, "Home on the Range"

Joy seems to be a product of the geography.
—**IAN FRAZIER**

Bountiful, UT, was one of the first out-settlements of the Church of the Latter Day Saints, taking its name from the harvest hoped for by the Mormon settlers. Charles Mabey, a native of this town, served as Governor of Utah from 1921–25. He ran unsuccessfully for a second term against George Henry Dern, who used the slogan "We need a Dern good governor and we don't mean Mabey." If the good people of Utah recognized genius when they saw it, then Dern was elected governor on the strength of that slogan alone.

The town of **Waterproof, LA**, is an example of misguided optimism, since more than once in its history it has been under several feet of water. In fact, due to the erosion of the river bank by the Mississippi River, the town has had to pick up and move a number of times. The original Waterproof now lies well out into the mighty Mississip'.

An owner of the local railroad, Tom Best, is honored by the name **Best, TX**. What started as a camp during the oil boom in Texas later became known as the town with the "best name and worst reputation." Southwest from Best lies **Blessing, TX**. A large landowner, intensely relieved that the railroad had arrived here, wanted to name the town "Thank God." Railroad officials rejected the name, apparently uneasy that conductors would announce the train stop by walking through the passenger cars shouting "Thank God, Thank God." Blessing was mutually agreed upon as an acceptable, if noticeably more restrained, substitution.

Harmony, PA, was the site of The Harmony Society of George Rapp. Adherents (almost all of whom had come directly from Germany to live in Harmony) owned all property in common, wore similar clothing, worked hard, and practiced celibacy, believing it would bring them closer to God. Later, they decided life would be more harmonious in Indiana, so they moved there. Unfortunately, many of them fell sick from malaria and the group decided that, on second thought, the Keystone State wasn't so bad. They returned to a different location in Pennsylvania and named their new settlement Economy. They didn't have to economize for long, however, because oil was found on their land and the group became immensely wealthy.

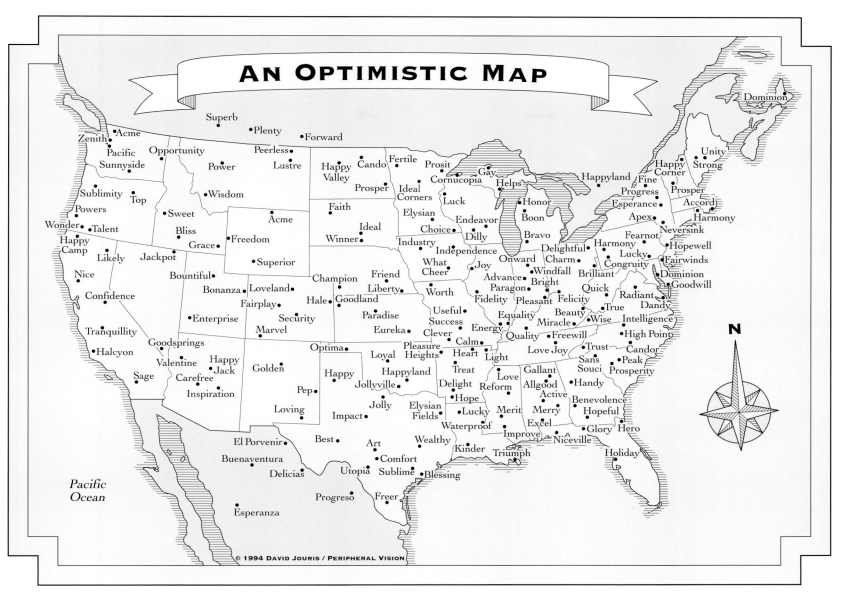

AN OPTIMISTIC MAP

Superb • Plenty • Forward
•Acme Peerless
Zenith Opportunity Lustre Happy Cando Fertile Prosit
Pacific Power Valley Cornucopia Gay Happyland Unity
Sunnyside Prosper Ideal Luck Helps Progress Happy Strong
Wisdom Corners Honor Esperance Fine Corner Prosper
Sublimity Top Faith Elysian Endeavor Boon Apex Accord Harmony
Powers Sweet Acme Ideal Choice Dilly Bravo Fearnot Neversink
Wonder Talent Bliss Winner Industry Independence Delightful Harmony Hopewell
Happy Grace Freedom What Joy Onward Charm Lucky Fairwinds
Camp Likely Jackpot Superior Cheer Advance Windfall Brilliant Congruity Dominion
Nice Bountiful Champion Friend Worth Paragon Bright Quick Radiant Goodwill
Confidence Bonanza Loveland Liberty Fidelity Pleasant Felicity True Dandy
Enterprise Fairplay Hale Goodland Useful Equality Beauty Wise Intelligence
Tranquillity Marvel Security Paradise Success Miracle High Point
Goodsprings Optima Eureka Clever Energy Quality Freewill Trust
Halcyon Valentine Happy Golden Loyal Pleasure Calm Light Love Joy Candor Peak
Sage Jack Happy Heights Heart Gallant Sans Prosperity
Carefree Pep Jollyville Happyland Treat Love Souci Handy
Inspiration Jolly Delight Reform Allgood Active Benevolence
Loving Impact Elysian Hope Merit Merry Hopeful
Fields Lucky Excel Glory Hero
El Porvenir Best Art Wealthy Waterproof Improve Niceville
Buenaventura Comfort Kinder Triumph Holiday
Delicias Utopia Sublime Blessing
Progreso Freer
Esperanza

Pacific
Ocean

N

© 1994 DAVID JOURIS / PERIPHERAL VISION

87

Egypt, TX, was the name given to a farming community after the citizens provided corn to needy farmers during a bad drought. Their actions were reminiscent of the Pharaoh in Egypt, who put aside grain during bountiful years as a means of assuring that his people would be able to eat during periods without rain.

The small community of **Africa, OH**, got its name during the mid 1800s when a number of the residents were active in the underground railroad that helped African-Americans escape slavery and oppression in the South. This town was a stop along the way to new beginnings in northern Ohio and Pennsylvania. One resident, however, disagreed with these actions, and named the town Africa with disparaging intentions.

Japan, MO, is so called after a local church that is dedicated to the Holy Martyrs of Japan. These martyrs were Christian missionaries who were looking for converts in Japan during latter part of the sixteenth century. Fearful that their country was being prepared for a foreign takeover, the Japanese martyred several dozen missionaries and followers near Nagasaki in 1597.

The town of **Canton, MA**, came by its name, the story goes, because its location was considered to be on the exact opposite side of the world from the like-named city in China. (Evidently, geography wasn't a strong subject in former times either.)

It should be noted that towns bearing well-known exotic names are sometimes affected by American individuality—leading to unexpected pronounciations: **Madrid, IA**, is pronounced MAD-rid; **Russia, OH**, ROO-she; Versailles, KY, Vur-SALES; Cairo, IL, KAY-row; Bremen, GA, BREE-mun; Vienna, GA, VI-enna.

The U.S.A. has its share of exotic structures, too. ***Stonehenge***, near Maryhill, WA, is a full-sized stone replica of the original in England. Speaking of England, ***Shakespeare's Globe Theatre*** in Odessa, TX, is a replica of the Globe Theatre that used to stand in London. In Kimballton, IA, a town where some 75 percent of the residents are of Danish descent, there's a statue of the ***Little Mermaid*** (in the park on Main Street) that is modeled after the famous one in Copenhagen. The ***Tower of Pisa***, in Niles, IL, is half the size of the one in Italy, and cleverly functions as a water tower for the YMCA next to it. Nashville, TN, has an full-scale replica of the ***Parthenon*** that serves as an art gallery and museum. And there is *one* exotic site in the United States, where an *original* structure stands—or spans. ***London Bridge***, at Lake Havasu City in Arizona, is the real thing, imported from London.

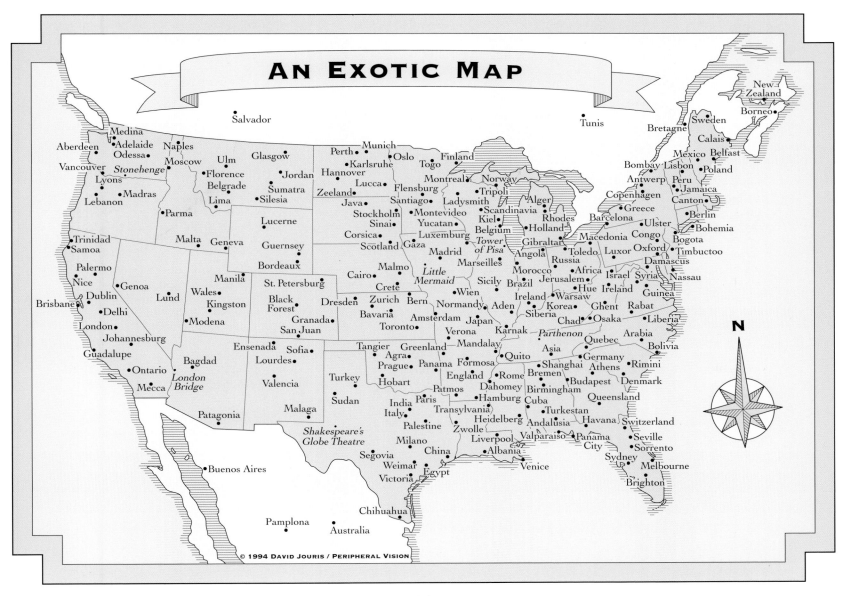

AN EXOTIC MAP

Confusion is a word we have invented
for an order which is not understood.
—**HENRY MILLER**

Anyone who isn't confused here
doesn't really understand what's going on.
—**ANONYMOUS**

Even more confusing than a town that appears to be a few hundred—or a few thousand—miles out of place is discovering two towns of the same name within a few dozen miles of each other. In Indiana, for example, there are two communities named Scipio—one named for the Roman general, the other for the chief of the Peoria Indian tribe—within sixty miles of one another. And to further complicate matters, one of those communities lies partly in Indiana, and partly in Ohio. Although there might be a number of places within a state that bear the same name, only one is allowed to have a post office bearing that name.

There are quite a number of names that appear over and over again as one looks at a map of the United States—towns like Franklin (not coincidentally, Benjamin Franklin was the first Postmaster General, as well as one of our Founding Fathers), Oakland, Fairview, Midway, Centerville, Oak Grove, Riverside, Five Points, Pleasant Hill. And it is not only town names that pop up repeatedly: at one time, Minnesota had at least a hundred bodies of water named Mud Lake. Alaska has a couple of interesting names that reveal two ways of dealing with the confusion created by repeated use of the same name. One is the throw-up-your-hands-in-desperation method that is evidenced by the name given by two geologists in the 1920s to a river in the south-central part of the state—Another River. The other employs the use-a-language-other-than-English method (and its corollary, the how-to-avoid-censorship method). The name Anak Creek, up in the very northern part of Alaska, employs the Inuit language for the kind of creek up which one does not wish to be, especially when one is without a paddle.

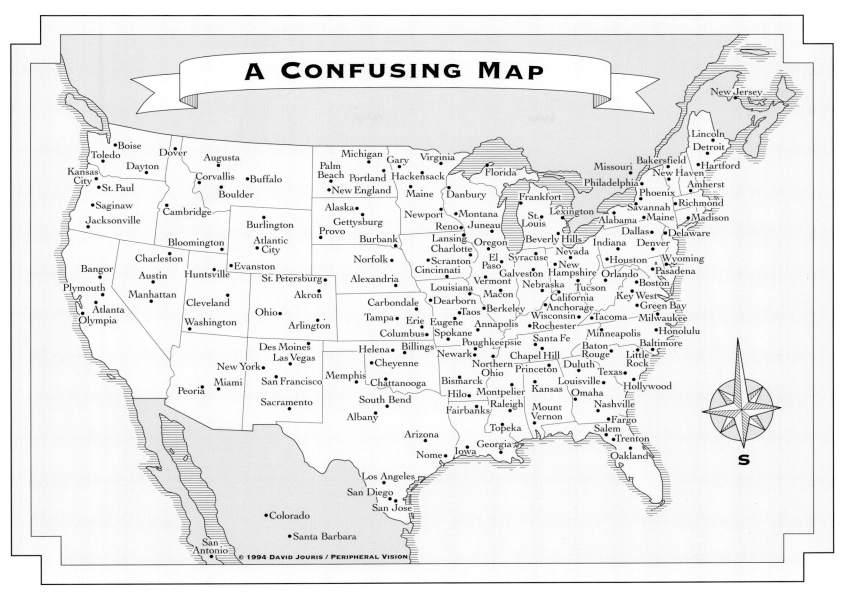

A CONFUSING MAP

© 1994 David Jouris / Peripheral Vision

S

Christmas is a widely observed holiday
on which neither the past nor the future
is of so much interest as the present.
—F. G. KERNAN

Christmas has not always been one of the United States' biggest holidays. In fact, the Puritans ignored all the holy days of the Church of England; the New England colonists passed a law in 1659 that anyone observing "any such day as Christmas" would be fined. This brings to mind H. L. Mencken's definition of Puritanism: "The haunting fear that someone, somewhere, may be happy." It wasn't really until the nineteenth century that Christmas began to be celebrated in New England.

Santa Claus, IN, was originally going to be named Santa Fe, but the residents found out there was already a town in Indiana with that name. Since it was nearing the Christmas season at the time, one of the locals jokingly proposed Santa Claus as a somewhat similar name. Residents liked the idea and got behind the new name with gusto. In Santa Claus, there are streets with names like Chestnut by the Fire, Ornament Lane, Herald Circle, Candy Cane Lane, Silver Bell Terrace, Noël Street, and Prancer Drive. The town even has a "Santa's Village," too, that is now part of an even bigger theme park named "Holiday World." Streets in newer subdivisions have taken names such as Good Friday Boulevard, Easter Circle, New Year's Eve Road, and so on. By the way, the local fire department truck, nicknamed "Rudolph," has a red light on the tip of its hood. The post office in town also serves as a remailing point for lots of Christmas cards—increasing the monthly volume of mail handled by the local post office from a norm of 15,000 pieces to more than 400,000 in December. A local group called Santa's Elves helps take on the task of answering children's letters, routed to the Indiana community from all over the country.

Christmas, FL, was named after a military post was set up there on December 25, 1837. **Christmas, AZ**, got its name because a miner found out his mining claim here had been confirmed on December 25, 1902.

There is a Donner und Blitzen River in Oregon, that brings to mind two of Santa's reindeer. (In Christmas literature, one finds both spellings for the seventh reindeer: "Donner" and "Donder.") The river was named by soldiers of German origin who crossed it during a storm, hence the name, which translates as "thunder and lightning." There was once a town called Voltage in this area, a name suggested by the first postmaster because he thought that sufficient "voltage" could be generated by the Donner und Blitzen River to serve the whole region. It has been suggested that the postmaster was not the first person to confuse force with power.

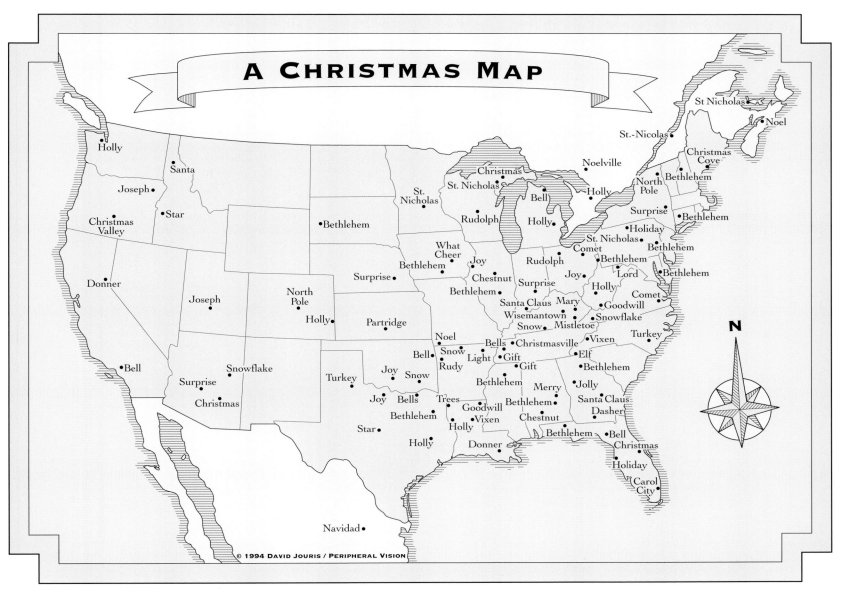

A CHRISTMAS MAP

Holly · · Santa · Joseph · · Star · Christmas Valley · Donner · Joseph · North Pole · Holly · · Bell · Surprise · Snowflake · Surprise · Christmas · Navidad · · Turkey · Joy · Snow · Joy · Bells · Star · Bethlehem · Holly · Partridge · Bethlehem · Surprise · What Cheer · Bethlehem · Joy · Chestnut · Bethlehem · Bell · Snow · Light · Gift · Gift · Bethlehem · Bethlehem · Trees · Goodwill · Vixen · Holly · Donner · Christmas · St. Nicholas · Rudolph · Bethlehem · Holly · Bell · Rudolph · Surprise · Santa Claus · Wisemantown · Snow · Noel · Bells · Snow · Rudy · Christmasville · Merry · Bethlehem · Chestnut · Bethlehem · Noelville · St. Nicholas · Holly · North Pole · Surprise · Holiday · St. Nicholas · Comet · Joy · Joy · Lord · Holly · Mary · Goodwill · Mistletoe · Vixen · Elf · Bethlehem · Jolly · Santa Claus · Dasher · Bell · Christmas · Holiday · Carol City · St Nicholas · Noel · St.-Nicholas · Christmas Cove · Bethlehem · Bethlehem · Bethlehem · Bethlehem · Comet · Snowflake · Turkey

N

© 1994 David Jouris / Peripheral Vision

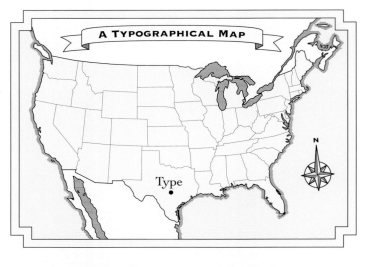

A TYPOGRAPHICAL MAP

Type

I am the leaden army that conquers the world—
I am TYPE.
—FREDERIC W. GOUDY

C O L O P H O N

Copperplate (used for the headlines): This typeface was designed in the early 1900s, with the original work being credited to Frederic W. Goudy, and with subsequent weights and widths done by Clarence C. Marder. There is, however, some suspicion that Goudy was simply following the instructions given to him by the American Type Founders Company, which had commissioned the work.

Cochin (used for the main body of text and for town names on the maps): This face, originated by Peignot foundry in Paris, about 1915, was based on the lettering style of the French copperplate engravers of the eighteenth century. It is named after a French copperplate engraver and artist, Charles Nicholas Cochin. (It should be noted that Cochin is a different typeface than the one named Nicholas Cochin.)

A BIOGRAPHICAL MAP

The Art of Biography
Is Different from Geography.
Geography is about Maps,
But Biography is about Chaps.
—EDMUND CLERIHEW BENTLEY

ABOUT THE AUTHOR

David Jouris was established in the mid 1900s. Originally sited in a farming region east of San Francisco, CA, the location has changed quite a number of times since then. In spite of a recently espoused theory that David Jouris was named for the sixteenth-century Dutch theologian David Joris, "an extreme inspirationist," the name was in fact chosen by Virginia Holstrom Jouris in honor of three like-named relatives. David Jouris is known for photographic postcards, greeting cards, and posters, as well as for mapmaking.

AN UPCOMING MAP

Next •

N

Even in a perfect world
Where everyone was equal,
I'd still own the film rights
And be working on the sequel.
— **ELVIS COSTELLO**,
"Everyday I Write the Book"

WHAT'S AHEAD?

In the works is another extraordinary atlas of the United States, featuring even more towns that actually exist. Already nearing completion are maps concerned with such themes as Architecture, Transportation, Gambling, Drinking, Fashion, Trees, Repetition, Mathematics, Shakespeare, American History, and Cheese.